TIME-TRAVEL MATH

TIME-TRAVEL MATH

AN ADVANCED GEOMETRY ADVENTURE FOR GRADES 4-5

AMY BERNSTEIN
ILLUSTRATED BY MICHELLE M. FARISS

Routledge
Taylor & Francis Group

NEW YORK AND LONDON

First published 2010 by Prufrock Press Inc.

Published 2021 by Routledge
605 Third Avenue, New York, NY 10017
2 Park Square, Milton Park, Abingdon, Oxon OX14 4RN

Routledge is an imprint of the Taylor & Francis Group, an informa business

Copyright © 2010 by Taylor & Francis.

Illustrations © Michelle Fariss
Edited by Kelly Dilworth
Cover and Layout Design by Marjorie Parker
Illustrated by Michelle Fariss

ISBN 13: 978-1-59363-413-1 (pbk)

TABLE OF CONTENTS

INTRODUCTION

In mathematical quarters, the regular division of the plane has been considered theoretically. . . . [Mathematicians] have opened the gate leading to an extensive domain, but they have not entered this domain themselves. By their very nature they are more interested in the way in which the gate is opened than in the garden lying behind it.

—M. C. Escher (1958, p. 156)

ABOUT THE BOOK

Time-Travel Math: An Advanced Geometry Adventure for Grades 4–5 is designed for students who have a high ability in mathematics. In particular, this book is designed for those students who are interested in "the garden lying behind" geometrical concepts. Gifted students often ask their teachers, "What is math for?" This book provides those students with some answers.

Throughout history, people have used geometry to solve a wide range of creative problems. *Time-Travel Math* helps students make this connection by closely examining the fascinating geometry behind three historic achievements: Leonardo da Vinci's accurate rendering of the human figure, M. C. Escher's geometry-based art, and Imhotep's Great Pyramid for the Pharaoh Djoser.

Time-Travel Math is divided into three cumulative units that may be reproduced by the teacher and handed out to students:
*   ★ Unit 1: Leonardo da Vinci and Ratio;
*   ★ Unit 2: M. C. Escher, Symmetry, and Angles; and
*   ★ Unit 3: The Egyptians and Area.

Each unit begins with a fictional time-travel story that is woven throughout the book. The narrative is then followed by a series of connected lessons that combine challenging written work problems with hands-on activities.

Why Time-Travel Math?

Time-Travel Math: An Advanced Geometry Adventure for Grades 4–5 is a unique literary-math hybrid that combines imaginative storytelling with challenging geometry lessons.

For those students who enjoy literary narrative, the time-travel math story that is woven throughout the book helps connect the work problems to one another and lends a personal flavor to the text. Many students like to find an emotional connection to what they are doing and will sometimes lose interest in math problems that lack that personal connection. This math activity book gives students who enjoy narrative the opportunity to connect geometry to real life and to think about math in a fresh light.

In addition, the lessons in *Time-Travel Math* challenge all students to strengthen their critical thinking, spatial visualization, abstract reasoning, and problem-solving skills in a new way by requiring students to think through advanced geometry problems as they read.

As students work through the lessons in the book, they will improve their mathematical literacy and renew their understanding of the relationship between history, art, language, and math. They will explore key geometry concepts such as ratios, angles, regular polygons, symmetry, and area in depth, and they will learn how to put those concepts to practical use.

Standards

Time-Travel Math incorporates the following National Council of Teachers of Mathematics geometry standards for grades 3–5 (NCTM, 2000):

In grades 3–5, all students should:

* identify, compare, and analyze attributes of two- and three-dimensional shapes and develop vocabulary to describe the attributes;
* classify two- and three-dimensional shapes according to their properties and develop definitions of classes of shapes such as triangles and pyramids;
* investigate, describe, and reason about the results of subdividing, combining, and transforming shapes;
* explore congruence and similarity;
* make and test conjectures about geometric properties and relationships and develop logical arguments to justify conclusions;
* predict and describe the results of sliding, flipping, and turning two-dimensional shapes;
* describe a motion or a series of motions that will show that two shapes are congruent;
* identify and describe line and rotational symmetry in two- and three-dimensional shapes and designs;
* build and draw geometric objects;
* create and describe mental images of objects, patterns, and paths;
* identify and build a three-dimensional object from two-dimensional representations of that object;
* identify and draw a two-dimensional representation of a three-dimensional object;
* use geometric models to solve problems in other areas of mathematics, such as number and measurement; and
* recognize geometric ideas and relationships and apply them to other disciplines and to problems that arise in the classroom or in everyday life.

Time-Travel Math also reinforces the skills standards suggested by the National Council of Teachers of Mathematics in the areas of communication, problem solving, and connecting math skills (NCTM, 2000).

How to Use This Book

Time-Travel Math is divided into three cumulative units that should be followed in order.

Each reproducible unit is preceded by a teacher's guide, which introduces the unit and gives a short overview of the lessons. The teacher's guide is then followed by the reproducible section of the unit, labeled by adventure, that can be photocopied in full and handed to students as one large work packet (similar to a workbook). You may also photocopy the lessons individually and hand out the lessons to students as they go along. Make sure that you hand out the lessons in order, however, because each lesson builds upon ideas that were introduced in the previous lesson.

If you are using the book in a regular education classroom, with a few students who have the need and the ability to go beyond the regular math curriculum, you may:

* Allow students to "test out" of the subject that the rest of the class will be covering for a few weeks or longer. (This is also known as curriculum compacting. For a description of this technique, and other ways to make sure that students know the needed material so that they can "buy time" for other activities, check out the revised edition of Susan Winebrenner's excellent book, *Teaching Gifted Kids in the Regular Classroom,* published in 2001 by Free Spirit.) Allow advanced students to replace the work that the class is doing with a section of *Time-Travel Math.* Read aloud the introductory story or allow students to read it independently. During times when the rest of the class is working in groups, spend an equal part of the class time with this group on discussion and problem solving. Let students work independently, or as a group, on the problems in class or for homework.
* Set up a Challenge Math Center, with sections of *Time-Travel Math* available. Let students work on sections of this book independently once they have demonstrated competency in the area in which they have chosen to test out.

If you are using the book in a classroom that is solely for gifted students, you may:

* Read aloud the introductory story or allow students to read it independently.
* Group the students in your class by level and allow them to work on the discussion and problem-solving sections together.
* Circulate among the groups to help facilitate discussion.
* Have students work independently on the problems in class or for homework.

If you are using this book as a parent at home, you may:

* Read the story sections with your child, and lead him or her in a discussion of the more difficult abstract thinking questions (see below) once your child reaches them. Allow your child to work through the

rest of the book on his or her own, and only provide guidance when needed.

No matter how you decide to use *Time-Travel Math,* let your students' curiosity be your guide. Don't be too quick to direct students to the "right" answers. Let them have fun!

The Stories. If you choose to hand students the lessons in pieces, rather than handing out each unit as one large work packet, make sure that you include relevant portions of the fictional stories along with the students' handouts. The stories are integral to the work problems and cannot be separated from the lessons. As students work their way through the problems in each unit, they will confront a wide variety of questions that directly relate to the ongoing story. Students will also rely on information gleaned through their reading to successfully complete the lessons in the unit.

Abstract Thinking Questions. This book is designed for students who have a high ability in mathematics. As a result, the book requires students to make some fairly large intellectual leaps now and then and intentionally does not provide the kind of step-by-step scaffolding that most of us would require for making these jumps.

You should expect your students to struggle through a number of difficult problem sets on their own. However, each lesson also includes several challenging, abstract thinking questions that may require additional guidance from a teacher or a mentor, or from a parent at home.

The abstract thinking questions appear each time that a new idea is introduced and are clearly labeled in bold letters. The questions are interspersed throughout the lessons and often depend upon the student's completion of earlier problem sets in order to be answered.

Ideally, when a student comes across a question labeled, **Abstract Thinking Question**, he or she will have an opportunity to discuss the question with a teacher or a mentor soon after the question appears. Verbally talking out his or her ideas about the question will help the student process the question more thoroughly.

If immediate discussion is not possible with an adult, ask students to respond to the question in writing and then set up a time in the near future when you or someone else can provide the student with some feedback. In addition, you may have participating students gather together and discuss the abstract thinking questions as a group.

If you prefer that students discuss the abstract thinking questions aloud before they move on to the rest of the questions in the lesson, then you may ask students to stop working on the lesson once an abstract thinking question appears. Students may then resume the lesson after they have discussed the question aloud.

Hands-On Activities. For each hands-on activity that appears in a lesson, materials needed for the activity are listed along with clear, easy-to-follow instructions. Most of the activities may be completed independently as students work their way through the book. However, some activities will require additional help from the teacher, or from a parent. Detailed instructions for the activities that require additional assistance are provided in the Teacher's Guide at the beginning of each unit. Additional instructions for the most labor-intensive activity in the book, the tessellation quilt, are included as a supplement in Appendix A.

Possible Adaptations. If you are working with a student who is gifted in mathematics but who struggles with reading, or if you are working with a gifted student with a learning disability, you may want to read aloud or tape record the text, stopping to pose questions and discuss the problems as you go along.

Or, depending upon the individual student's needs, you may want to send the reading-intensive portions of the book home with the student so that he or she may prepare for the next day's lesson the night before. In the latter case, make sure that the student waits for the opportunity to discuss the work problems in class.

Assessment

At the back of this book, you will find a detailed answer key for both the work problems and the abstract thinking questions (see Appendix B), as well as selected rubrics for some of the more complicated hands-on activities (see Appendix C).

Assess for understanding by periodically collecting students' lessons as they work their way through the units. Pay close attention to students' answers when discussing the abstract thinking questions and give students clear deadlines for turning in products such as drawings and constructions.

If a student is working through the book at an independent pace, make sure that you assess his or her progress before you allow the student to move on to the next unit.

UNIT
1

LEONARDO DA VINCI AND RATIO

Art is supposed to just be creative, right? Not using measurements or math or anything like that.

—Harriet

TEACHER'S GUIDE

About the Unit

For this unit, students will travel back in time with fictional math whizzes, Harriet and Thomas, to 15th-century Renaissance Italy. There they will meet a young Leonardo da Vinci who is having trouble drawing human figures with the right proportions. Students will then follow along as Harriet and Thomas try to use math to solve Leonardo's problem.

As students work through the lessons in the unit, they will investigate proportions, ratio relationships, averages, and more. By the time that they finish the unit, students will have a solid understanding of the nature of ratio and they will be able to put their newfound knowledge to practical use by drawing and building objects to scale.

Skills

Ratio is, by its nature, a challenging math topic for elementary-aged students to master. Because it is about relationship, it requires a level of abstract thinking that basic computation does not. Students with a high ability in mathematics are often ready for this kind of thinking at an earlier age than their peers. They enjoy the abstract thinking that the problems require, and they are capable of taking the large leaps of thought that the problems ask of them.

Skills that students will need to have prior to completing this unit include addition, subtraction, multiplication, and division of whole numbers and halves; rounding to the nearest whole number; measuring in inches; and reducing fractions.

About the Lessons

Lesson 1.1: Ratio. For this lesson, students will investigate the nature of ratio and create their own definition of a ratio, limiting what a ratio relationship can be.

Lesson 1.2: Measuring Body Parts. For this lesson, students will measure and compare the relationship between body part sizes. Students will then represent their answers using drawings and symbols. Ideally, students will work together in pairs so that they can measure one another for the lesson. However, a student working alone can measure a friend or classmate instead. The suggested answers for this lesson (which can be found on pp. 122–123 in Appendix B) are not the only answers possible, but instead indicate the direction in which students should be going. Question 6 is the most difficult question in the lesson, as students must figure out that ¼ is the same as 1:4.

Lesson 1.3: Averages. The previous lesson ended by teaching students about the abstract concept of "average" and how the average helps to ascertain whether something is generally true, rather than just true of a specific individual. This lesson builds upon Lesson 1.2 by having students work with the practical application of finding an average.

Lesson 1.4: More Ratios. For this lesson, the students must figure out how to use ratio to create furniture to scale. Students are given the size of a real human figure and the size of an object in the real world, and they must then decide upon the scale for those objects and use the scale to design a desk for a much smaller figure. As an extension, students may create a model of the tiny desk out of paper and tape.

Lesson 1.5: *The Giant Hand.* For this lesson, students will go in the other direction with ratio by making an object become much larger, rather than smaller. As students work through the lesson, they will have to figure out on their own how to reverse the process that they used for the last lesson. Students will also have to figure out on their own that in order to proceed with the lesson and figure out the ratio between a person's height and his or her foot size, they will need to use the previous answers from their chart.

Lesson 1.6: *Drawing Proportions.* For this lesson, students will reduce drawings by a certain ratio using a grid. Check to see if they kept the proportions the same in their drawing.

Lesson 1.7: *Making a Giant Object Group Project.* For this lesson, students will put their knowledge of ratio relationships to practical use by building a giant object to scale.

This project is optional because it requires that a group of students work on it together. (Otherwise, if a student tries to work on the project alone, the project will take too long to build and the math thinking will get lost in the construction time.) If you can gather a group of students together, then I would recommend trying it as students often enjoy this project a great deal.

Before your students begin working on the project, look at the object that the students pick and make sure that it is small and fairly simple in shape. Remember that the model will be 24 times the object's true size. Ask for help from parents or from an art teacher with gathering materials and with constructing the object. Some objects that have worked well for my students in the past include a Coca Cola can, a penny, a dollar bill, a notebook, an iPod, a candy bar, a pencil, an eraser, a pad of paper, and a cell phone. Make sure that the math is correct in the scale drawing before any construction begins.

Extra Challenge. This optional extension can be used as an alternative to Lesson 1.7 or as a supplement. For this project, students will draw your classroom to scale. Students may work alone or in pairs on this project.

THE FIRST ADVENTURE

Harriet often wondered after her inquisitiveness got them into their first great adventure what would have happened, or rather not happened, if it weren't for her unstoppable curiosity. Maybe she and her twin brother, Thomas, would have just continued to live normal lives like other children.

After all, without Harriet and her insatiable curiosity, Thomas would definitely have quit once the adventure began to look just a little bit sketchy and dangerous. And then that would have been the end of everything! Thomas was great at solving a puzzle once he knew exactly what the problem was, but he never went looking for trouble in the way that his sister did. Nothing stopped Harriet, though, once she began to wonder about something. It was Harriet's best—and worst—characteristic.

On that memorable summer day, Harriet and Thomas spent the whole morning drawing figures. For some reason, all of Harriet's figures came out looking strange. The figures' hands were too big for their arms and their heads looked like they might topple right off of their skinny necks. Nothing was right. Thomas' drawings were strange too. His figures looked like they could walk across rivers on their too-long legs. The twins tried and tried to fix the drawings, but they finally gave up.

"I wonder how artists figured out the right way to draw people," said Harriet. "Clearly someone must have figured it out."

"Wonder on," said Thomas, looking in dismay at their drawings.

Later that afternoon, the twins wandered around their neighborhood on the Upper West Side of Manhattan. Being native New Yorkers, they were allowed quite a bit of freedom to explore the city on their own, as long as they carried a cell phone and checked in with their parents every now and then.

Thomas and Harriet's parents were scientists who often worked late hours and trusted the children to take care of themselves. Recently, the twins' parents had given Thomas a smart phone that connected to the Internet. The phone was small, sleek, and silver.

The two children loved to wander around the streets of New York City. They always found something new and interesting to investigate. On that sunny summer day, they visited The Dakota apartment building, which had always been one of their favorite buildings.

The Dakota was home to many of New York City's oldest and wealthiest families. It was an enormous old building that surrounded a large courtyard. For many years, Thomas and Harriet passed by the courtyard on their way to Central Park and wondered what it looked like inside.

It was a challenge for them to sneak inside the courtyard because the guards at the gate kept a sharp look out for trouble (and children who wandered around the building were definitely considered to be "trouble"). But Harriet and Thomas soon found a way to outsmart the guards. They learned that the guards had a regular route that they had to follow every hour. So, if they just waited long enough, the guard on duty would walk across the courtyard and be gone for 75 seconds while he looked around a far corner to make sure that nobody was lurking there. This was Thomas and Harriet's cue to hotfoot it past the guard booth, and into the courtyard, where they could duck down behind a parked car and wait until the guard returned to his guard booth. Then, it was simply a matter of scooting across the courtyard one at a time while the guard wasn't looking, and then running toward the same corner that he had just been examining a few moments ago. Here, they found their favorite spot. When they looked three stories up, past the apartment windows, they could see their favorite gargoyle in the city.

This particular gargoyle was a statue of the head of a bearded man wearing a crown. On either side of the gargoyle lurked two angry dragons that were each biting hard on the railing. Harriet thought that the dragons looked as though they would release their grip and breathe fire as soon as she approached. The gargoyle too looked less than friendly. His eyes were closed and his mouth was grim. But for some reason, Harriet and Thomas had always liked all three of the figures. They often wondered what would happen if they were ever able to climb up to where the figures were; but there had never seemed to be a way to do it.

Today, however, Harriet noticed a set of steps for the first time. They were chipped roughly from the grey stone of the building and they led directly to the gargoyle. Harriet could have sworn that they had never been there before and Thomas agreed. Nervous about what Harriet might do, Thomas suggested that they forget about the steps and just go home. Steps that suddenly appear out of nowhere could only lead to somewhere dangerous.

As Thomas turned toward the courtyard entrance, Harriet reminded him that he always wanted to quit just at the moment when things got interesting. She decided to ignore him and began to climb. Not wanting to leave her, Thomas reluctantly followed.

It was surprisingly difficult to climb the rough stones. Adding to the difficulty was the children's fear that the guard might look up and see them, especially now that they were in plain sight high above him. What if someone just happened to look out of an apartment window at this moment? Then what would they do?

Harriet and Thomas just kept climbing. Harriet reached for the gargoyle first. "Don't touch it," warned Thomas. But it was too late. Harriet had brushed the gargoyle with her fingertips. Suddenly, there was a great flash of light and Harriet was sure that she was going to fall. She clutched at Thomas' arm. What was going on?

The stone gargoyle opened his eyes and stared at the children. Then, he opened his mouth and stretched his thin red lips, letting escape a deep groan. The two dragons, which suddenly had grown enormous, stopped clutching the iron railing with their teeth and turned their no-longer-stone green heads around to blink at the children with lively, bright yellow eyes. Steam puffed out of each dragon's mouth.

The gargoyle parted his lips and smiled a ghastly kind of a smile. His teeth still looked like grey stone, but his tongue was now bright red. He cleared his stony throat.

Harriet and Thomas gripped the walls as hard as they could and tried not to drop to certain death in the courtyard below. They looked at each other in shock. The gargoyle spoke.

"You were wondering something?" he asked in a calm but gravelly voice. There was a silence. Then Harriet realized that he was addressing them.

"What?"

"You two, you were wondering something," he said again.

"We were?" asked Harriet.

"Earlier, yes, you were wondering something," he said kindly and pleasantly. "Put your hand on my beard for the answer."

"Answer to what?" asked Harriet.

"What you wondered . . . about the drawings."

"What?" gasped Harriet, still feeling confused.

"Put your hand on my beard!" His voice was starting to sound cross.

"Now, wait just a minute," begged Thomas. But Harriet already had leaned forward toward the no-longer-stone grey beard. Harriet reached for the beard and touched it. She never could wait, once she was curious. As soon as she touched the beard, the dragons' mouth erupted with fire, and there was another flash of light, and then . . .

Suddenly, the twins were standing in a cobblestone street. The gargoyle and the dragons had disappeared and so too had the apartment building.

Wherever the twins were now, it sure didn't look like New York City. All along the street were tiny workshops. In one workshop, the twins could see a man pounding sheets of iron. Behind him hung pieces of armor that looked like the ones that knights had once worn. Next door to the man pounding iron was another man sitting at a desk with a book propped up in front of him. The man was slowly copying the book onto paper with a quill pen. In a third doorway, the twins could see two people putting together complex parts of what looked like a clock.

The strangers were all very oddly dressed too. The men were wearing tights and tunics and weird puffy hats.

Harriet listened as one of the clock makers spoke to the other in a language other than English.

"Where are we?" she asked.

"More to the point, when are we?" replied Thomas.

Harriet realized that he was right. They were not only in a completely different place than they had been a few minutes ago. They also seemed to have gone somewhere else in time.

People didn't make armor or copy books with a quill pen in Thomas and Harriet's time. They lived in the time of computers and cell phones and on-demand television. Just then, Harriet got an idea. "Try your cell phone," she suggested.

"I don't think Mom or Dad are going to know the answer to this one," replied Thomas.

"Just check the date," said Harriet. But when Thomas pulled his phone out of his pocket, he just stared at it. The phone was no longer silver. Instead, it was now dark red velvet and was covered with bright jewels on the numbers. The phone showed an image of a dragon on the screen. The dragon looked like one of the gargoyle's two friends.

Thomas flipped the phone open cautiously and poked the button for calendar. In a quiet voice, he read what it said out loud. "October 16, 1456, Florence, Italy."

Thomas continued reading. "Please press button number two if you want to be able to understand Italian." Thomas looked at his sister.

"Now what?" he asked.

Just at that moment, a boy approached the twins politely as they stood there in the street. (At least, Harriet thought he was a boy. He had long hair like a girl, but she remembered reading that boys wore their hair long in the Renaissance period, the time that they were apparently now in.)

The boy appeared to be about 12 years old. He started talking a mile a minute at Harriet and Thomas while bowing low and sweeping his hat off of his head. They couldn't understand a word he was saying.

The boy grabbed onto Thomas' sleeve and began pulling him into one of the shops, waving at Harriet to follow. Inside the shop, the boy let go of the sleeve, but he continued waving his hands frantically, signaling the twins to follow. He then led Harriet and Thomas over to a low table.

On the table were huge pieces of drawing paper covered in fine ink drawings. The boy picked up a quill pen and gestured to the drawings with it. He then pointed to himself.

Harriet had never seen such drawings. She blushed, remembering the pictures that she had tried to draw this morning. This boy was an incredible artist! His drawings were beautiful; the lines were so delicate and skilled.

The boy was still yammering at them in Italian. It seemed that something was wrong. Thomas bent over to take a closer look at the drawings.

"Hey!" he said. "He has the same problem that we do."

"What?" asked Harriet.

She looked at the drawings again. They were beautiful, yes, but the pictures of people looked strange. Just like in her and Thomas' drawings that morning, the figures in the drawings also had legs that were too long, or arms that were too short. One woman's head was huge for her body. A man had hands as big as his head. The twins could see that the boy was not happy with this situation.

Suddenly, Harriet remembered what the gargoyle had said. He had asked her, "You were wondering something?"

Earlier that morning, they had wondered about the sizes of body parts in their drawings and questioned who had been the first person to figure out how to draw people correctly, and when it had been done. Now, here they were in the distant past, in Italy, and someone was trying to solve the exact same problem.

"I think we are supposed to help this boy solve his problem," she told Thomas.

"Ok, I'm willing to try," Thomas replied logically, "but we can't even talk to him."

The boy was still speaking in Italian and gesturing at the drawings. Then Harriet remembered the cell phone. She grabbed it from her brother and pressed number two.

"And if I turn in these drawings looking like this, I will lose my job as an apprentice, and then what shall I do?" asked the boy.

"We can understand you!" exclaimed Thomas.

"Well, of course you can. I was speaking quite clearly," the boy said, frowning. "Anyway, I can't get these drawings to have the right **proportions**. If I can't figure out a better way to draw them, I will lose my job."

"Hello," said Harriet, trying to slow him down a bit. "My name is Harriet and this is my brother Thomas."

"Leonardo," he said, impatiently, pointing to himself.

"Not the Leonardo?" asked Thomas. "Leonardo da Vinci?"

"Who?" asked Harriet.

"Yes, I am from Vinci," said Leonardo. "But about my problem . . . "

Thomas stared at Leonardo in disbelief. "You're Leonardo da Vinci, the great Renaissance artist, inventor, mathematician, writer, botanist, scientist, writer, and musician, to name just a few?"

"I am just an apprentice artist who is about to lose his job," replied Leonardo.

"I've heard of you," interrupted Harriet. "Didn't you invent the first helicopter and paint the Mona Lisa?"

"What's a helicopter?" replied Leonardo.

"He hasn't done any of those things yet" said Thomas, "and he may never get to do them if he doesn't figure out his drawing problem and become a successful artist."

"I have to get these people to have the right proportions," said Leonardo.

"Well, what do 'proportions' mean?" asked Thomas sensibly. He always got right to the heart of a problem.

"That means . . . you know—the sizes of things and how they fit together. Like having the right sized leg for a person in a drawing so that it looks real. Or drawing people so that their arms and heads are all the proper size."

"Oh, well, we're not too good at that either," noted Harriet.

"Yeah, we really messed up our own drawings this morning," said Thomas. There was a silence.

"We could measure someone, a real person. Then we could figure out the **ratio** between our different body parts, using math, and make all of our drawn people fit those rules. Then they would look right," said Harriet. "But I guess that would be cheating, wouldn't it? Art is supposed to just be creative, right? Not using measurements or math or anything like that."

That's why she thought that she could never be really good at art. She liked to do things logically and mathematically.

Leonardo stared at her. "That's brilliant!" he screeched.

He threw his arms around her and gave her a bear hug. "What is a ratio?"

"It's a relationship between two things expressed as a number," said Thomas.

"What?" asked Leonardo.

"Ways that things relate to each other as numbers can be expressed as a ratio," said Harriet. "For example, take the sizes of things. When you say, 'He is twice as tall as his dog,' that is a ratio. If he is 4 feet tall and his dog is 2 feet tall, the ratio would be 4:2, which is the same as 2 to 1—you can always simplify ratios, just like fractions, by dividing both numbers by the same number. Or, take temperatures. If it is 90 degrees outside, and it was only 30 degrees in January, that would be a ratio of 90:30, which is the same as 3 to 1. You always use the lowest possible numbers while keeping the ratio the same," said Harriet. "But you can't express other kinds of relationships as a ratio because they don't use numbers. You can't express a relationship between two friends, or how happy you are, as a ratio."

"I can," said Thomas. "Take this, for example: I am twice as happy as I was this morning when we were trying to draw people."

"You can't say you are exactly twice as happy, because you can't count happiness—that's just impossible," said Harriet. "Ratio does not tell you which of two people is friendlier or prettier or wiser. You can't express those relationships in numbers. Ratio *can* tell you the relationship between the sizes of two objects. If you hear someone say, 'That tree is three times as big as you are,' and you know that you are 5 feet tall, then you can figure out that the tree is 15 feet high. You and the tree have a 1:3 height ratio."

"We need to help Leonardo figure out the ratios between the sizes of the parts of the human body," said Thomas.

"We can make ratios for body part sizes," said Harriet.

"Yes! It may just work!" cried Leonardo.

"Of course it will work," said Thomas. "My sister is a genius."

"Leonardo is the genius," answered Harriet.

"That will work, it really will!" Leonardo yelled in excitement. "Let's start with ourselves! I will measure you first, Thomas."

"Alright," said Thomas as he stretched his arms out like the letter, T, waiting for Leonardo to measure him.

LESSON 1.1: RATIO

1. **Abstract Thinking Question.** Ratio can express many relationships besides ones about size. Can you think of other kinds of relationships that can be expressed as a ratio? List some possible ratio relationships.

2. **Abstract Thinking Question.** List some kinds of relationships that cannot be expressed as a ratio.

3. Can a relationship between two people's strength be expressed as a ratio?

4. Here is an example: Samantha is twice as strong as Susan. If Susan can lift 75 pounds, how many pounds can Samantha lift?

5. What mathematical operation did you use to figure out the answer to Problem 4?

6. ***Abstract Thinking Question.*** How did you know how many times to multiply 75?

7. If the relationship between Norman and Bob's shoe size is 1:4, and Norman wears size 2 shoes, what size shoe does Bob wear? (The ratio is always given in the same order as the subjects, so 1:4 means Norman: Bob.)

You might have "just known" the answer to Problem 7. But what did your brain do to figure it out? You might have thought, what is the same to 2 as 4 is to 1?

In order to figure out ratios using higher numbers, you need to understand the mathematical process you go through in your mind in order to apply a ratio to a specific number and create steps.

Here's one way you might do it:

★ First, you make the **ratio** into a fraction in your mind. 1:4 equals ¼. The 1 represents Norman's shoe size and the 4 represents Bob's shoe size. Keeping numbers in the same order is important.

★ Create an **equation** that begins with the ratio fraction and ends with the fraction containing the number that you know. Remember that the fraction with the number that you know (Norman's real shoe size) must be equal to the ratio fraction. Write an = sign between the two fractions. For the second fraction, the 2 should be in Norman's place and so your equation should look like this: ¼ = 2/x

★ Then, divide the larger numerator (2) by the smaller numerator (1). 2 divided by 1 = 2.

★ Next, multiply the known denominator (4) by the result: 4 × 2 = 8

★ Put the 8 in place of the unknown: ¼ = 2/8.

★ Convert your fraction into a ratio, 2:8, and determine your answer: Bob wears size 8 shoes.

★ Remember that you can use a similar process if the known number is the denominator.

8. What would you do if you knew Bob wore a size 8 shoe, but you didn't know what size shoe Norman wore, and the ratios were the same?

9. *Extra Credit.* What is the root of the word **equation**?

LESSON 1.2: MEASURING BODY PARTS

Harriet and Leonardo discovered some interesting **ratios** by measuring the different parts of Thomas's body. They recorded their findings on the chart below. They used a colon (:) between any two numbers in a ratio.

1. Can you turn Harriet and Leonardo's findings into pictures and then into equations? After you are done, check to see if your equations are correct by measuring yourself. Write your answers in the boxes. The first one has been done for you. Remember that in the "test it out" column, your answers will vary.

LEONARDO AND HARRIET'S IDEAS ABOUT THE SIZE RELATIONSHIPS OF BODY PARTS

Leonardo and the twins discovered that:	How might you draw it?	How could you write it as a number sentence using letters as symbols?	Test it out on yourself or with a partner. Is it true?	Ratio between parts:
1. If a person spreads out his or her arms, the distance from the end of one hand to the end of the other will be equal to that person's height.		H = height A = outspread arms H = A	Yes, it is true! My arms together are 5'1" inch long, and that is my exact height!	1:1
2. The length of the foot from the end of the toes to the heel goes twice into the distance from the heel to the knee.				

Leonardo and the twins discovered that:	How might you draw it?	How could you write it as a number sentence using letters as symbols?	Test it out on yourself or with a partner. Is it true?	Ratio between parts:
3. From the tip of the longest finger of the hand to the shoulder joint equals four hands.				
4. From the tip of the longest finger of the hand to the shoulder joint equals four faces.				
5. The thinnest part of the leg in profile goes five times into the distance from the sole of the foot to the knee joint.				
6. When kneeling, a person loses one fourth of his height.				

2. ***Abstract Thinking Question.*** Did you find that some of your answers in the "test it out" column were the same as Leonardo and Harriet's answers and some answers were different? Most people do. Do you have an idea of why that might be? Explain.

After Harriet and Leonardo had made all of the measurements of Thomas, they decided to try the same measurements out on themselves. To their surprise, not all of their answers were the same.

"I got totally different answers from you two. Look, two times my arm length is not the same as my height at all," said Harriet.

"Mine is, and look, so is Leo's—Do you mind if I call you Leo?" Thomas asked Leonardo.

"Not at all," answered Leonardo, "all of my friends do."

"Ours are the same, but yours is different. Maybe it's because you are a girl."

"But four of my hands doesn't equal the distance from my finger to my shoulder," said Leo, "and yours do, Thomas, and we are both boys."

The rules didn't work out to be the same on all three of them.

"The third one is true for me, about the arm length equaling four hands," said Harriet.

"And for me too," said Thomas.

"Not for me at all," said Leo.

"Does this mean our method can't work?" asked Thomas.

"How are we going to make true rules for drawing if everyone is different?" asked Thomas.

"Oh no," worried Leonardo. "I am going to lose my job after all." He slumped down onto the ground.

"Don't give up," said Thomas, "we'll think of something."

Leonardo looked glumly at the ground. He began drawing in the dirt with a stick. This guy really liked to draw. Harriet saw a very skinny, tall, young man come walking along the road. Leonardo began to draw him. He muttered, "Arm length equals height . . . " But when Harriet looked at the guy walking by, she could see the rule wouldn't work for him.

"How can we have rules if they don't apply to everyone?" asked Thomas.

Harriet watched a short, chubby woman trundle by pushing a cart. Leo drew her, muttering, "Arm length equals height?" This rule seemed to be true for the woman, but would the foot rule work on her?

"How can our rules be true if they don't exactly fit everyone?" Harriet wondered, echoing Thomas.

3. ***Abstract Thinking Question.*** Can you think of some possible reasons for the differences between Harriet, Thomas, and Leonardo's body part ratios?

LESSON 1.3: AVERAGES

"I know!" said Thomas after a while. "We have to figure out what is mostly true. There is a regular size for bananas, but there are tiny bananas and huge bananas. You wouldn't draw weird-sized ones, unless you wanted to specifically draw huge or tiny bananas. You have to figure out what sizes are the most *generally* true!" said Thomas.

"That's right! We need to figure out the **average**!" yelled Harriet.

"What's that?" asked Leo.

"If you measure the body parts of a crowd of people, they will each have slightly different measurements. After that, you need to figure out the middle measurements. Then you will know what is most regular, and that is what will look normal!"

"Yes," said Thomas. "That's it! And the more people we measure, the more correct our drawing rules will be."

"I see," said Leo. "You are saying that the middle will be the most common. Then we must go out and measure a whole bunch of people right away," said Leonardo. And so the three set off to measure as many people as they could find.

Leonardo and the twins measured tall people and short people, young people and old people, girls and boys. Then they found the averages for all of the body part ratios that they had been trying to establish.

Here is what they found out when they measured the people in Leonardo's town:

	Frederico	Io	Paulo	Natalie	Philip	Bella	Sam	Maria	Tim	Christina
Height	5'5"	6'	4'6"	5'8"	4'10"	4'	3'4"	5'6"	2'6"	4'8"
Arm span	60"	72"	53"	70"	52"	61"	38"	64"	30"	56"
Foot length	7"	9"	7"	8"	7"	7"	6"	9"	4"	7"
Heel to knee	15"	18"	13"	17"	14"	15"	11"	17"	8"	14"
Hand	6"	8"	5"	6"	6"	7"	4"	7"	3"	5"
Finger to shoulder	26"	32"	22"	27"	24"	29"	18"	28"	13"	22"
Face	6"	8"	5"	6 ½"	7"	6"	4"	7"	3"	5"
Leg width	3"	3"	3"	3"	3"	3"	2"	4"	2"	3"

Then, they took this data and found the middle number for each body part measurement so that they could set up their rules.

Can you do what they did?

Start out by finding the middle measurement for each body part on the chart. There are several kinds of middle, but in this situation, you need to find the **average** or **mean** number for each measurement. This will tell you what is usual, or ordinary, for that part of the body's size.

Here's how you find an average. First, you add together all of the instances of height.

1. But wait! Before you do that, you have to turn the measurements into just inches, instead of mixed inches and feet. How do you change mixed feet and inches into just inches?

Once you have added up all of the heights, divide that number by the number of people in your group, in this case, 10. You can round your answer to the nearest whole number.

2. The average height for this group is:

3. Find the average arm span in the same way that you found the average height. Show your work. The average arm span is:

4. What is the ratio between the average height and the average arm span?

Are they equal, as Leo and Thomas' theory says that they should be? If so, the ratio would be 1:1 because one arm span equals one height for the average person.

5. Fill in the chart below for the people in Leonardo's town:

	Average		Average
Height		Hand	
Arm span		Finger to shoulder	
Foot length		Face	
Heel to knee		Leg width	

6. Are Leo's theories correct? Fill in the chart below:

Leonardo and the twins discovered that:	Ratio	Is this statement true for the average person in Leonardo's town? Show your work.
If a person spreads out his or her arms, the distance from the end of one hand to the end of the other will be equal to that person's height.	A = Arm span H = Height A = H	
The length of the foot from the end of the toes to the heel goes twice into the distance from the heel to the knee.	F = foot length K = knee to heel 2:1 = F:K	
From the tip of the longest finger of the hand to the shoulder joint equals four hands.	A = arm from fingers to shoulder H = hands 1:4 = H:A	

Leonardo and the twins discovered that:	Ratio	Is this statement true for the average person in Leonardo's town? Show your work.
From the tip of the longest finger of the hand to the shoulder joint equals four faces.	F = faces A = arm from fingers to shoulder 1:4 = F:A	
The thinnest part of the leg in profile goes five times into the distance from the sole of the foot to the knee joint.	K = knee to heel L = leg width 1:5 = L:K	
When kneeling down, a person loses one fourth of his height.	K = knee to heel H = Height 1:4 = K:H	

7. Leonardo and the twins are right about the basic ratios of body parts to one another. Why do you think one of the ratios is not exactly as Leonardo and the twins thought it would be?

8. If the number of people measured (**the sample**) were larger than 10, do you think the answer would be closer to or further from what the children thought it would be? Explain why.

9. Make a chart and measure the body parts of the people in your class. Find the averages and decide if the children's theories hold true for your classmates. You may have to round your numbers to the nearest inch.

LESSON 1.4: MORE RATIOS

As soon as Leonardo had all of the rules he needed, he tried them out in a drawing. His drawing looked like this:

"It's perfect!" cried Leonardo. "Now I will be able to become an artist. Thank you so much!"

"Oh, it's nothing," said Thomas.

"Just run-of-the-mill brilliance," said Harriet.

Leonardo smiled. "How can I thank you?"

"No need to thank us," said Thomas.

"You can give us that drawing," interrupted Harriet.

So Leonardo wrapped up the beautiful drawing of the girl and handed it to Harriet. He hugged them both and thanked them again. Then he ran off into his shop to get back to his artwork before his master became angry with him. The children were left standing in the street, holding the picture. Meanwhile, the sky had clouded up while they were helping Leonardo and now it began to rain. Harriet hid Leonardo's picture under her sweatshirt to keep it dry. The twins stood under the eves of one of the shops and looked at each other.

"Well," said Thomas, who always got to the point of things, "I think it is time to go home."

"Yes," agreed Harriet. "But how?" It was raining harder now and getting a bit chilly, as well. Harriet realized that she had eaten nothing since breakfast. Her stomach grumbled. "Yooo, hoo, gargoyle!" she called out feebly. Nothing happened. "Hey!"

Still nothing.

"I don't think I want to just stay here," said Thomas. "I mean, it's very nice and all, but I miss my computer."

"And our parents, of course," said Harriet.

"Of course," said Thomas, looking glum.

Suddenly, Harriet's face lit up. "The phone!"

"That's right!" exclaimed Thomas. He pulled the phone out of his pocket.

Sure enough, there was a green jewel on the face that was labeled, "Home."

"Push it! Push it!" shouted Harriet.

"But will we be able to come back again?" asked Thomas.

"I don't know," answered Harriet as the clouds began to thunder, "but I think it is time to go."

A bolt of lightning shot through the dark sky.

"Grab onto my arm," shouted Thomas. The thunder began to pound even louder. Harriet grasped a bit of sleeve as Thomas pushed the green button. Suddenly, there was a bright flash. "Is it lightning or time travel?" Harriet wondered. And then . . .

The twins looked around and then at each other. They were standing again at the gates of The Dakota and the guard was looking at them with suspicion.

"Move along home now, children," he said gruffly. The twins nodded and walked home.

On their way home, Harriet and Thomas looked at the picture of a girl drawn by Leonardo according to their new rules for ratio and proportion. It looked perfect to them.

They named the girl in the picture, Maria. When they returned home, Harriet placed the drawing on the shelf and stared at it. It would be fun, she thought, if she created a paper doll version of Maria with the same proportions as the drawing. But first she would need to build a room for

Maria to live in and furniture for Maria to use. Harriet enlisted Thomas for help. The twins knew that Maria's furniture would be the same size for Maria, as Harriet's is for her. Maria's furniture would have to be the same **proportion** to her as Harriet's furniture is to Harriet. Otherwise, it would be too large or too small for Maria to use.

The twins figured out the size of Maria's furniture using **ratio** again. Ratio, remember, is the relationship between two things expressed as a number. Any ratio is also the same as a fraction. 1:2 is the same as ½.

1. ***Abstract Thinking Question.*** Can you figure out how tall Maria's desk has to be for the proportions to be correct? Remember that Maria's desk height is the same ratio to Harriet's desk height as Maria's height is to Harriet's height. Harriet's height is 5' tall. Harriet's desk is 3' tall. How will you figure this ratio out?

   Write out the steps you would use to figure out the height of Maria's desk at her tiny school if you knew that the ratio of Maria's height to her desk height was the same as Harriet's height to *her* desk height. Round the numbers to make it easier. The first step has been done for you.

   Step 1: First, I would measure Leonardo's drawing of Maria on page 25.

2. Now figure out Maria's desk height. Show your work.

Answer: Maria's desk height would be _____

Time-Travel Math © Prufrock Press • Permission is granted to photocopy or reproduce this page for classroom use only.

Name: _____ Date: _____

EXTENSION

Materials

* several sheets of paper
* scissors
* tape
* pencil
* a piece of furniture in your classroom or home

Procedure

* Turn to page 25 in your work packet and cut the drawing of Maria out.
* Make a tiny desk for Maria to use out of paper and tape. Use your classroom desk as a model.

1. What would the desk's length and width be?

* Pick another piece of furniture to create for Maria.
* Use your own height and a piece of furniture (a bed, a table, a chair) from your house or classroom.
* Use the ratio you figured out for Harriet's desk. Show your work.

2. What would the piece of furniture's length and width be?

LESSON 1.5: THE GIANT HAND

Knowing what you do now about ratios and proportions, try this puzzle:

The villagers outside of the town where Leonardo lives claim they have a giant living in their mountains. They know that the giant exists, because one day, when they entered the village square, there was a giant footprint across the marketplace. The villagers claim that the giant crushed all of the market stalls and left a footprint 14 feet long.

1. **Abstract Thinking Question**. How tall is the giant? Explain how you will go about figuring this out. Show your work. (Hint: Use the measurements of the people in Leonardo's chart for which you found the averages in Lesson 1.3, Problem 5 to find the heights you need. Use averages and ratio.)

   Step 1:

   Step 2:

   Step 3:

   Step 4:

2. Now solve it! The Giant is _____ tall.

LESSON 1.6: DRAWING PROPORTIONS

Harriet had a class assignment for science. She had to bring in a picture of a human face and show its parts. She remembered the drawing that Leonardo had given her, and thought how cool it would be to bring in part of this drawing (the part that shows the face). Harriet had to copy that part of it by hand. She only wanted the face and she wanted the face to be as big as possible so that everyone in her class could see it. As you can see, the face in this drawing is small. Luckily, she now knew how to make a larger copy, but still keep the drawing the same proportions.

Here's what Harriet did:
* First, Harriet measured the face. It was 4" in height, by 2" in width.
* Then, she decided what she wanted the ratio to be between the original drawing and the new big drawing. She wanted the ratio to be 1:6. (So one inch in the original would be 6 inches in the final drawing.)
* Next, Harriet drew a grid over the original face drawing. She divided it into 8 equal parts. She used light pencil so that she could erase it without messing up the drawing.

* Then, she made a larger grid where each square is 6" by 6" and there are still 2 × 4 squares.
* She transferred one square of the drawing at a time, so that each square in the large picture was exactly the same as the matching square in the small drawing.

1. Can you transfer each square of the drawing just as Harriet did? Harriet drew her face directly on a grid that she created herself. However, another way that you might do it would be to draw each box on an individual sheet of paper and then tape the boxes together to form a face. Try it.

Materials

* ★ several sheets of drawing paper.
* ★ scissors
* ★ tape
* ★ a ruler
* ★ a pencil
* ★ markers, crayons, or colored pencils (optional)

Procedure

* ★ Take a sheet of drawing paper and, using your ruler and a pencil, draw a 6" by 6" square. Cut it out.
* ★ Continue cutting out 6" by 6" squares until you have a total of eight squares.
* ★ Draw Maria's face by transferring one square at a time. As you transfer the squares, check to make sure that the squares match up when you place them side-by-side. You may want to place a square next to the last one that you finished before you begin drawing a new square.
* ★ Once you are finished transferring the squares, turn the squares over and tape them together so that they form one large reproduction of Maria's face.
* ★ *Optional.* Decorate your drawing by coloring in the squares.

LESSON 1.7: MAKING A GIANT OBJECT GROUP PROJECT

Materials

* ★ one small object
* ★ several sheets of paper for brainstorming and drawing
* ★ a pencil
* ★ art materials for building the object

Before you begin your project, ask your teacher about the availability of materials in your classroom.

Procedure

1. Together with your group, find a small object that you would like to make large enough so that the giant from Lesson 1.5 can use it. The object can be a pencil, a coin, an iPod, a ruler, a Coca Cola can, or any other small, simple object.
2. Together with your group, brainstorm a list of objects that are not too complicated, but not too simple either, that a giant might need. Assume that this giant is about your age.
3. Ask your teacher to look at the list and narrow it down to objects that she or he thinks it is possible to make. Then, vote as a group on which object you will build for the giant. (Hint: Do you remember the **scale** for the giant?)
4. Before you begin building your object, you will first have to create a full-sized, scale drawing of your object with all of the measurements labeled. In the space provided on the following page, record the steps that you will take to make a full-sized drawing of your object. Make sure that you explain how you will accomplish the math that is involved.
5. Have the steps approved by your teacher before you begin drawing. Then, draw your object to scale. Once you have completed your scale drawing, allow your teacher to check it.

6. Once your scale drawing has been approved, begin planning your giant object. What materials will you need to build the object? What will you do first, second, and third? Write down the steps that you will need to complete in the space below.

Steps:

EXTRA CHALLENGE: DRAW A MODEL OF YOUR CLASSROOM

Materials

* several sheets of drawing paper
* pencil

Procedure

1. Using the same ratio that you used for Maria's desk in Lesson 1.4, draw a scale model of your classroom.
2. First, go back to the problem that refers to the size of Maria's desk. What was the ratio between Maria's world and our world?
3. Next, draw a scale drawing of a classroom for Maria. Make her room the same shape as your classroom. Label all wall measurements.
4. Use your classroom as a model and copy it in Maria's scale.

Example:

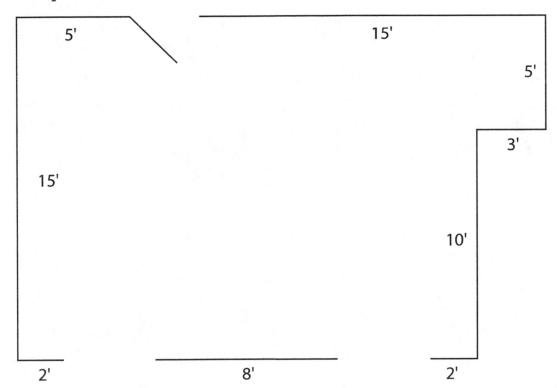

GLOSSARY

Average: A quantity that is usual, determined by adding together examples and dividing by the number of the sample.

Equation: A mathematical statement that says that two expressions are equal.

Mean: See Average.

Proportion: The comparison in size of parts to a whole.

Ratio: The comparison of two things that can be expressed by a number. Ratio shows how many times one quantity is contained in another.

Sample: The group selected to represent the whole population in research.

UNIT
2

M. C. ESCHER, SYMMETRY, AND ANGLES

Math is used in practically everything!

—Harriet

TEACHER'S GUIDE

About the Unit

For this unit, students will travel back in time with fictional math whizzes, Harriet and Thomas, to early 20th-century Holland. There they will meet a young M. C. Escher who is having trouble drawing tessellations. Students will then follow along as Harriet and Thomas try to use math to solve M. C. Escher's problem.

As students work through the lessons in the unit, they will investigate the geometry of angles and regular polygons. By the time that they finish the unit, students will have a solid understanding of the geometry used to create tessellation art. Students will then be able to put their newfound knowledge to practical use by creating their own tessellations.

Skills

Skills that students will need to have prior to completing this unit include knowledge of the concept of angle measurements and the names of regular polygons.

About the Lessons

Lesson 2.1: Symmetry. For this lesson, students will investigate the meaning of the complex concept of symmetry and they will learn why the definition of symmetry can mean more than just a mirror reflection.

Lesson 2.2: Planes. For this lesson, students will work with plane figures, lines, and polygons. As they work through the problems in the lesson, students will think about why shapes have certain names and what it means that something "goes on forever."

Lesson 2.3: Polygons. For this lesson, students will learn the names of particular polygons and their meaning.

Lesson 2.4: Tessellations. For this lesson, students will play with shapes and try to figure out why certain regular polygons tessellate and others do not. (The angles of the shapes that tessellate must evenly add up to 360.)

Lesson 2.5: Tearing Triangles. For this lesson, students will engage in further experiments to figure out why certain regular polygons tessellate and others do not. If students already have figured out that certain regular polygons tessellate because 360 degrees is evenly divisible by their angle measurement, then they may skip this lesson.

Lesson 2.6: Translation Tessellations. This lesson is an opportunity for students to use what they have learned to make actual tessellation art. After cutting squares out of paper, students will adapt these squares in symmetrical ways so that the combined squares make interesting shapes that will still tessellate. Students can prepare for the activity by cutting small index cards into evenly sized squares. The students will need scissors, tape, and large drawing paper for this activity. As an extension, students may decorate their finished tessellations either by creating patterns with color or by coloring in the tessellation so that it looks like something recognizable.

Lesson 2.7: Rotational Symmetry Tessellation. For this lesson, students will take the idea of symmetry a bit further and create shapes that tessellate by rotating around a point. Students can use the same sort of squares to begin with as they used in the last packet. As an extension, students may decorate their finished tesselations.

Lesson 2.8: Tessellation Final Project. For their final project for this unit, students will complete two finished, creative tessellations. You may use the rubric found on page 136 (Appendix C) for evaluation purposes and also to explain the project expectations. If you wish to extend the project further, you may also assign for extra credit the challenge of making at least one of these tessellations using a triangle or a hexagon rather than a square.

Optional Group Project: Tessellation Quilts. For this project, each student will create his or her own tessellating square from fabric. Then, all of the squares will be assembled together into a tessellation quilt. These quilts are very beautiful when made out of real fabric. Children must be old enough to be quite competent with handling sharp scissors to participate in this project.

Note: The birds and fish drawing that Harriet and Thomas find on the Internet on page 42 is M. C. Escher's well-known woodcut, Sky and Water I. The image is widely available and easy to find online should you want students to view it.

THE SECOND ADVENTURE

Although Harriet and Thomas ventured back to The Dakota apartments many times in the next several weeks, nothing happened again. They would sneak past the guards and stand underneath the gargoyle and dragons, and look up at the stone figures with longing. But the strange stairway that led to the gargoyle was simply not there. The stairway stubbornly kept not being there with each visit, no matter how much Harriet wished to go on another adventure.

Of course, without the stairway, there was no other way for Harriet and Thomas to reach the top of the courtyard and touch the gargoyle's beard. Harriet was sure that all they had to do to be transported again was to climb up to the top of the courtyard and grab on to that beard. Then they would find themselves back with Leonardo, or wherever they wanted to go, whenever they wanted to go. But Thomas wasn't so sure.

"Maybe something special has to happen first to create the magic. I'm sure that not just any kid can go up that staircase at any time and grab that beard and be in Renaissance Italy, or wherever they want to be," Thomas whispered this to Harriet one day when they were standing underneath the gargoyle at The Dakota for about the 10th time that week.

"Of course, not just any kid," Harriet answered. "It has to be us."

"But why us?" Thomas asked with annoying reasonableness. "We are just regular kids. Maybe it was just our turn that day. Maybe it has happened to other kids before and will happen to other kids again, but we had our turn. Maybe we just happened to be in the right place at the right time and we never will be again."

Sometimes, Thomas's common sense was just a bit too much for Harriet.

"That is a terrible thought!" she told him. "Not just any kids would sneak past the guards at this building. Not just any kids would have the courage to climb up that staircase. But mostly, not just any kids would have been able to use math to help Leo with his problem! We were there in order to help him. I'm sure of it!"

"Maybe we were there because what we had been wondering about earlier that day was the same thing that Leo was wondering about," said Thomas.

"Hey, yeah!" shouted Harriet. "I forgot about the wondering. We have to wonder about something again!"

"Shhh," whispered Thomas. "The guards!"

"I wonder if the world is really flat?" Harriet whispered. She looked up. Nothing happened.

"I wonder if it will rain tonight?" asked Thomas in a loud voice.

"Shhhh," said Harriet. Still, nothing happened. "I don't see how wondering about the weather tonight can make any magic happen," said Harriet in an irritated voice. "I mean, how can the weather tonight be a problem for someone in another time and place? I was hoping we would be with Chris Columbus or Amerigo Vespucci or someone like that if we wondered about the flat Earth. But that didn't work."

"Maybe it has to have math in it," said Thomas. "You know, maybe is a math magic thing."

"Math is used in practically everything!" said Harriet.

"I wonder what the square root of 4 is?" Thomas said quietly.

"It's 2, because 2 times 2 is 4," said Harriet.

"I know that. I was just trying to wonder about something mathematical," answered Thomas.

"That was not real wondering then if you already knew the answer," said Harriet. "I wonder what 43,925 times 5,299 equals."

Nothing happened.

"232,758,575," said Thomas. He had his cell phone on calculator mode.

"That's not the right kind of question either, I don't think. If a person can answer the question with a machine, or a paper and pencil, then he doesn't really need our help," said Harriet.

The cell phone rang. Thomas tried to stifle the sound so that the guard wouldn't hear it. The twins scurried past the guard while he was on his rounds and answered the phone outside the building. It was their mom, asking if they would please come home for dinner now. They had to go.

The next day was a Saturday. Instead of going right over to The Dakota as they had been doing lately, the twins finished their breakfast quickly and began to search on the computer for something that might take them back in time again.

On a whim, Harriet entered a search for Leonardo da Vinci, and there, right in front of them, were extensive examples of their friend's art and inventions.

"How weird to read about someone you met who was a kid at the time, growing up, inventing things, becoming famous . . ."

"With our help, of course, which is never mentioned on any of the websites . . ." said Thomas.

"And then becoming part of the past," Harriet continued.

"Yeah, very strange," said Thomas.

"It says here that he was left-handed," said Harriet. "I didn't notice that, but it makes sense." Harriet was left-handed.

"I don't see why," answered Thomas, who was right-handed.

"Well, it just seems that many creative, artistic people are left-handed."

"But not all of them," Thomas protested.

Harriet entered a search for left-handedness into the computer. She came upon a website with a drawing of birds and fish that formed one unified picture without any gaps. The picture was both beautiful and surreal. The birds looked as if they were gradually turning into the fish, but there wasn't any overlap between the two creatures.

"Wow, look at those weird fish!" cried Harriet.

"And the birds too. Look at the birds!" answered Thomas.

"How did he do that?" Harriet wondered aloud. She took out some paper and fiddled around with making fish and birds that turned into each other. Nothing that she drew looked like these drawings at all.

"I wonder if math would help with this art too," said Thomas.

"I don't see how it could," answered Harriet. "I don't see what these drawings could have to do with math. But wait, you just wondered something. Do you think that maybe the gargoyle might be working again?"

"Let's go see," said Thomas. He leapt up from the computer and, remembering to grab his cell phone (which had returned to looking like a regular cell phone), followed Harriet out the door. They ran all the way uptown to 72nd street and Central Park West to their favorite building.

When they got back to The Dakota, they waited, as usual, for the guard to walk his path across the courtyard and look around the corner. Then, they ran past the guard booth and into the courtyard, ducked down behind a parked car, and waited until the guard returned to his booth. Then, they slipped across the courtyard one at a time when he wasn't looking and looped around the corner. From there, they could see their friend, the gargoyle.

He looked asleep up there, and also made out of stone, just like the last time they had been here. The dragons too were frozen and stiff.

"No, no magic," said Thomas with a sigh.

Then Harriet saw the steps. There they were again, little steep steps leading up to the top of the building. And this time, she was absolutely sure that they had not been there the last time that they had looked up.

"Eureka!" she shouted.

"Your what?" asked Thomas.

"No, Eureka! It means I have found it! It's Greek, or something like that. Look, the stairs are back." Harriet pointed to the stairs.

"Wait," said Thomas before Harriet could begin her climb.

"What?" asked Harriet.

"Wait," he said again.

"Why? Why wait?" she asked.

"I just think we should . . . It might be dangerous," answered Thomas.

"Didn't we just do all that stuff so that we could time travel again?" asked Harriet.

"Yes," said Thomas.

"So, there are the stairs, and at the top is the gargoyle. There is his beard . . . what's there to wait for? The wondering worked."

"Umm," said Thomas. Harriet began to climb. Thomas followed her, shaking his head and saying, "Ummm," all the way up to the top. When they arrived, the dragons let go of the railing that they had been clenching with their sharp teeth and turned toward the twins.

Just like the last time, the gargoyle opened his eyes and smiled at Thomas and Harriet with his grey stone teeth. He then licked his grey lips with his red tongue. The dragons glared at the twins with their piercing yellow eyes.

"May I grab your beard please?" asked Harriet politely. The gargoyle grinned.

"Of course," he said in his booming voice, "that's what I am here for!"

Harriet reached out a careful hand and gently touched his beard. As she did this, Thomas grabbed hold of her other hand. There was a flash, a boom and then . . .

Suddenly, they were standing in a strange city street. The street was less narrow than the streets in Leonardo's time and place, and everywhere they looked, there were canals and little boats. The houses nearby were very tall and narrow and each was a different color brick from its neighbor.

"Where are we this time?" asked Harriet.

"How about when are we?" replied Thomas. He took out his cell phone. Now it was shaped like a wooden shoe, with buttons that looked like little windmills fastened all over it.

"I think we're in Holland," he ventured. He flicked one of the little windmills and a date appeared on the screen. "In 1913."

"So, who are we supposed to meet here?" asked Harriet. There was no one around. They waited.

Then, a bedraggled and unhappy looking young man of about 15 came running along the bank of the nearest canal. When he got to a place about 10 yards from them, he stopped and picked up a big rock. He walked over to the canal and threw it in. Glumly, he watched it sink to the bottom.

"How about him?" said Harriet. "He looks like he needs help."

She walked right over to the young man and began talking to him. Of course, he couldn't understand a word that she was saying. He tried to answer her, but he was speaking Dutch so she couldn't understand him either. Thomas brought the phone over and flicked another windmill. The phone did its magic again and soon they could all understand each other.

"You sure don't look very happy." Harriet got right to the point. "Is there something wrong? Can we help?"

The boy looked up from the canal. He sighed. "I was just expelled from high school," he said. "I failed my exams."

"Oh dear," said Thomas, "I don't know how we can help with that."

"That's not really the problem," the boy said. "The problem is that I can't get my drawings to work the way that I want them to." He pulled a wad of papers out of a pocket as he said this and showed them to the twins.

They recognized what they saw immediately. There were fish turning into birds and lizards spiraling across the page. They looked kind of like the drawings Harriet and Thomas had been wondering about that

afternoon, but not as good. The patterns didn't quite work out. Harriet noticed that the boy was holding his papers in his left hand.

"Are you M. C. Escher, the famous artist?" asked Harriet.

"Maurits Cornelis Escher, at your service," he said, bowing. "But not at all famous. And you are?"

"Harriet and Thomas," they answered.

"I try, but I can't get my drawings to work right," he said. "So I will probably never be famous."

"I bet that's what we're here for," Harriet said to Thomas.

"Obviously," replied Thomas.

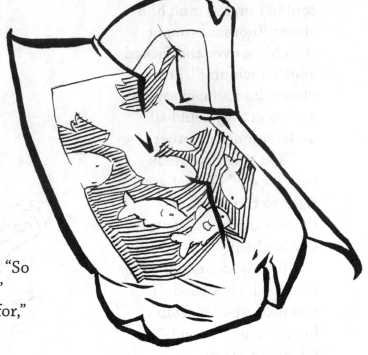

LESSON 2.1: SYMMETRY

"I have a feeling that these shapes can fit together in a beautiful way, but I just can't get it to work," he said.

"Explain it to us, please," said Harriet.

"Well, you see," Maurits began. "I am trying to make a new kind of picture that uses many of the same shapes all together. I need them to fit together without overlapping or leaving any gaps, even when I change the shape to make it look like a bird or a lizard. I keep putting these pentagons together, but it just doesn't work. See?" He showed them the sketch.

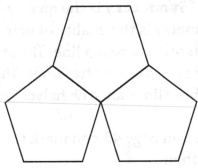

Harriet and Thomas could see that it didn't work. But they really didn't know what to suggest.

"Maybe, use another shape?" suggested Harriet.

"But which one?" asked Maurits.

"I think you better tell us a bit more," said Thomas.

"To help me, you have to first understand **symmetry**," said Maurits. He showed Harriet and Thomas a group of shapes that he had drawn on a sheet of paper and pointed to only some of them.

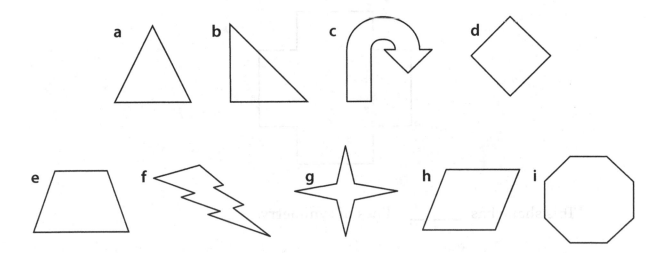

"These shapes here each have **line symmetry**," he said, tapping on the selected shapes as he illustrated his point.

"I know what line symmetry means!" said Harriet.

1. What do you think Harriet's definition for line symmetry might be?

"Right," said Maurits. "**Symmetry** is the quality of having exactly identical parts. Line symmetry is the quality of being made up of exactly identical parts facing each other across a line. The shapes that we have just looked at have symmetry across one or two lines. That means that you could fold the shape on these lines and the halves would match up exactly."

2. Go back to the shapes on page 47 and mark the lines of symmetry on each shape that has them.

3. Which shapes have more than two lines of symmetry?

4. How about this shape? How many lines of symmetry does it have? Draw the lines of symmetry.

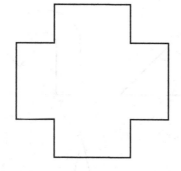

This shape has _____ lines of symmetry.

5. How many lines of symmetry does this shape have?

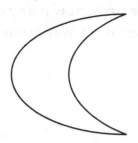

This shape has _____ lines of symmetry.

"Now, to make matters more complicated," Maurits went on, "there is another kind of symmetry called **rotational symmetry**. A shape that has rotational symmetry is exactly **congruent** with itself when it is **rotated** less than all the way around a central point.

Remember that all shapes will be identical to themselves if you **rotate** them all the way around. All the way around a circle is a turn of 360 degrees. If you turn any shape in a full circle, it will come back around to match up with itself again."

Maurits showed the twins this example of a shape turned 360 degrees around:

"But some shapes match up when you turn them only *part* of the way around. Halfway around a circle is 180 degrees. If a shape matches up after being turned 180 degrees around, it has **rotational symmetry.**

6. If all the way around a circle is 360 degrees, and halfway around is 180 degrees, how many degrees is it to go just one quarter of the way around?

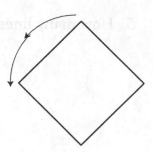

7. If half the way around a circle is 180 degrees, and half the way around a clock face is 30 minutes, what is the relationship between degrees and minutes on a clock's face?

One minute equals how many degrees?

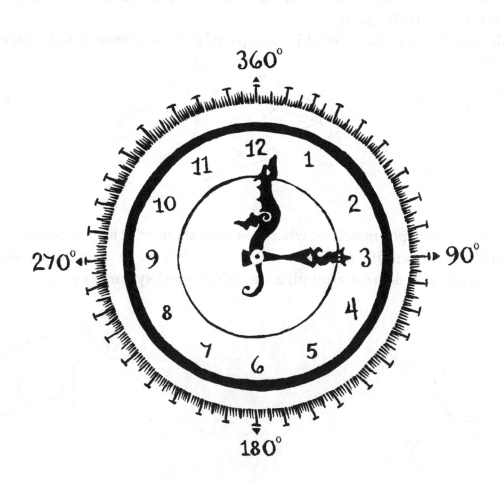

Draw the time markings and the hands of the clock for each problem below and explain your answers.

8. What is the angle (in degrees) for the hands of a clock at 1:20?

   What is the degree measurement for the other, larger angle?

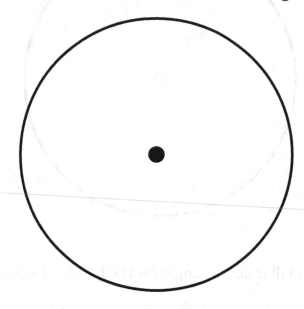

9. What is the smaller angle (in degrees) for the hands of a clock at 2:25?

   What is the degree measurement for the larger angle?

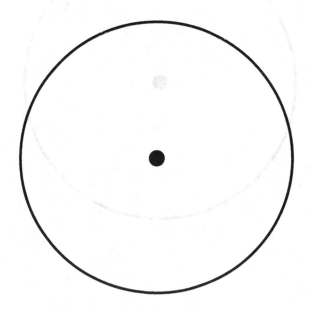

10. What is the degree measurement for the hands of a clock at 3:45?

What is the other angle's degree measurement?

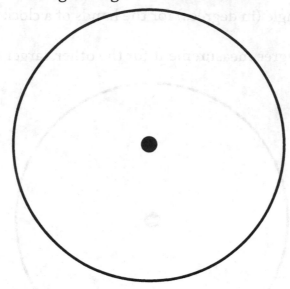

11. What is the smaller degree angle for the hands of a clock at 5:45?

What is the larger angle's degree measurement?

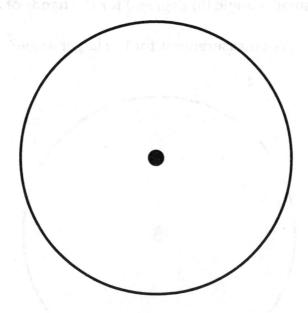

12. What is the smaller degree angle for the hands of a clock at 10:00?

What is the larger angle's degree measurement?

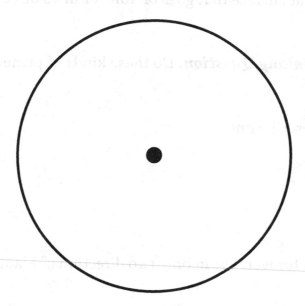

13. Observe the measurements that you have just made. What is the mathematical relationship between the measurements of the two angles in each clock?

Harriet looked at Maurits and frowned. "That is all okay," she began impatiently, "but what does it have to do with the problem that you're trying to solve?"

"Well, in order to help me solve my problem, you also have to understand **planes**," said Maurits.

"I don't think those are invented yet," said Harriet.

"Yes, they are," said Thomas. "The Wright Brothers would have invented the airplane 10 years before this time. But I don't think that's the kind of planes he means."

LESSON 2.2: PLANES

"A **plane** is a flat surface that goes on forever in all directions," said Maurits.

1. ***Abstract Thinking Question.*** Do these kinds of planes really exist on Earth?

    If they do, describe one.

"**Lines** also go on forever, but in only two directions," Maurits continued to explain.

"**Line Segments** are lines that do not go on forever. They have a certain length."

"**Plane Figures** are shapes that are drawn on a plane. They do *not* go on forever. They have a specific length and a specific width, but they have no depth. They are **two-dimensional**."

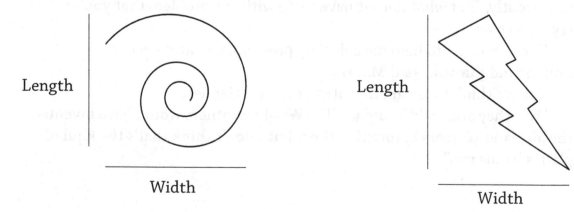

"**Polygons** are plane figures that are closed and have straight line segments and angles," he finished.

2. Draw a polygon that has lines instead of line segments.

3. **Abstract Thinking Question.** Why must plane figures be made up of line *segments* instead of lines?

4. What is the smallest number of line segments that you can have and still make a polygon from them?

5. What is the least number of angles you must have to make a polygon?

6. *Poly* comes from a Greek word that means "many." *Gon* comes from a Greek word that means "angles." What does the prefix *tri*, as in triangle, mean in mathematical terms?

7. What does the prefix *hexa,* as in hexagon, mean?

8. What does the prefix *octa,* as in octagon, mean?

9. What does the prefix *penta,* as in pentagon, mean?

LESSON 2.3: POLYGONS

1. Write the correct names on each of these polygons:

a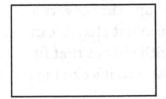

b

c

d

e

f

g

h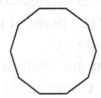

2. A regular polygon has all equal sides and angles. How many of the above shapes are **regular polygons**?

LESSON 2.4: TESSELLATIONS

"All right, I get all that," said Harriet. "Now can we try to fix your problem?"

"Okay, **tessellation** is my name for a repeated shape that covers a **plane** without any gaps or overlaps. My question is: What shapes can tessellate? And why? I can only make my artwork with shapes that fit together in this way. I don't know what shapes to use and it's driving me crazy!"

"Well," said Harriet, "I think we should try a shape out to see if it can tessellate."

"We might have some luck with triangles," ventured Thomas.

DRAW YOUR OWN TESSELLATION

Materials

* scissors
* pencil

Procedure

* Cut out the triangle below.
* Place your triangle in the middle of page 60 so that one of the triangle's points touches the tiny dot.
* Trace around the triangle using a pencil.
* Now, pick up the triangle and place it right next to the one that you just drew so that the point of the triangle again touches the dot. Trace around the triangle.
* Pick up the triangle again and slide it next to your last triangle. Continue tracing triangles side by side around the dot. Make sure that the **vertex** of the triangle is always on the dot. Keep tracing until you have completed the circle and have reached your first triangle.

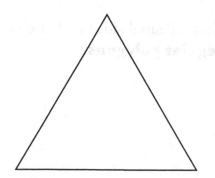

1. How many triangles did you draw around the point without any gaps or overlaps?

2. Congratulations! You have begun your first tessellation. Using the same triangle and tracing it many times, can you continue the pattern across the page until it fills the paper? Try it.

Time-Travel Math © Prufrock Press • Permission is granted to photocopy or reproduce this page for classroom use only.

3. **Abstract Thinking Question.** Of all regular polygons, how will you figure out which ones tessellate and which ones do not? You know now that triangles tessellate. They can fill up the plane without overlapping or leaving any gaps in between them. Predict which other regular polygons will tessellate the plane and which will not.

4. **Abstract Thinking Question.** Why do you think so? Explain.

5. **Abstract Thinking Question.** Which regular **polygons** do you think won't tessellate?

6. **Abstract Thinking Question.** Why don't you think they will tessellate? Explain.

TEST YOUR ANSWER

Materials

* one to two sheets of blank drawing paper
* scissors
* pencil

Procedure

* Cut out the shapes below.
* Choose one shape that you have cut out and place it on a blank sheet of drawing paper.
* Trace the shape, pick it up and place it directly next to the shape that you just traced, and then trace it again.
* Try to cover a sheet of paper with your shapes without leaving any gaps or creating any overlaps. Only use examples of the same shape and size together.
* Repeat this activity with each shape.

7. Can all of the shapes tessellate? Chart your findings on page 63.

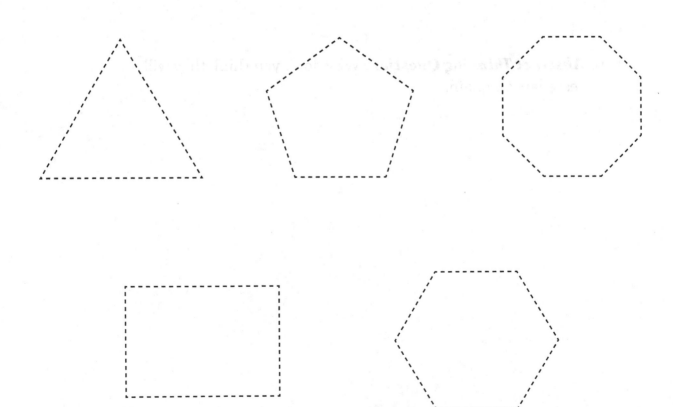

Chart your findings about tessellating shapes.

Shape	Yes, it can tessellate	No, it cannot tessellate
(triangle)		
(rectangle)		
(pentagon)		
(octagon)		
(hexagon)		

8. Were you correct in your prediction about which shapes will **tessellate**?

9. If you were correct, explain why you knew these would be the only tessellating regular polygons. If you were not correct, can you say now why these regular polygons tessellate and others do not?

LESSON 2.5: TEARING TRIANGLES

1. **Abstract Thinking Question.** Make the following prediction. If you were to tear off all three corners of any equilateral triangle (a triangle with all equal angles and sides,) and line the corners up along the line below, with their vertices all together in the middle of the line, do you think any space would be left between them on the line?

Try it.

Materials

* scissors

Procedure

* Cut out the triangle below.
* Tear off the triangle's three points.
* Line the points up so that the vertices all touch the dot on the line above.

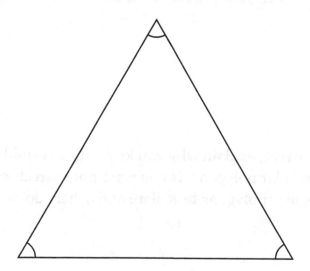

2. Did the triangle's points leave any spaces?

3. How many degrees are there in one angle of an equilateral triangle?

4. How many degrees are there in a straight line?

5. If you try the same experiment with the two non-equilateral triangles below, will the angles all fit on the line without leaving any gaps?

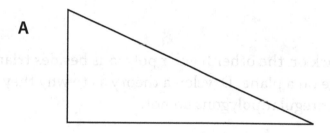

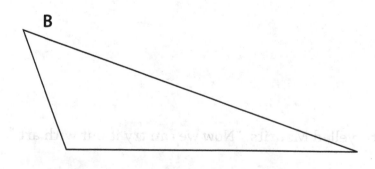

6. Predict the answer for Triangle A. Will all of the angles fit together on the line?

7. Predict the answer for Triangle B. Will all of the angles fit together on the line?

8. Now test your prediction. Cut out the two non-equilateral triangles on page 65. Tear off the corners. Put the triangles together on the line so that the points meet. Did all of the angles for each triangle fit together on the line without leaving a space?

9. Why do you think this is true?

10. Think back on the other regular polygons besides triangles that tessellate on a plane. Develop a theory as to why they tessellate and the other regular polygons do not.

"I get it!" yelled Maurits. "Now we can try it out with art."

LESSON 2.6: TRANSLATION TESSELLATIONS

For this lesson, you will learn how to modify a tessellating shape by **translation** (sliding).

Materials

* ★ 4" by 6" index card
* ★ ruler
* ★ scissors
* ★ pencil
* ★ multiple colored pencils, crayons, or markers
* ★ tape

Procedure

* ★ Start with a square. You know that a square will tessellate.

1. If you change the square in a symmetrical way, will it still tessellate?

* ★ Create the square by taking a 4" × 6" index card and, using a ruler, mark, then cut, a 4" × 4" square. For example, your index card should look like this:

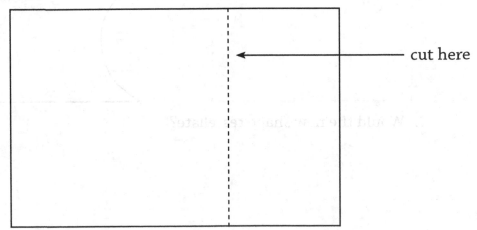

cut here

★ Observe your square. Suppose you change the square by adding a bump to one side. For example, your new shape might look like this:

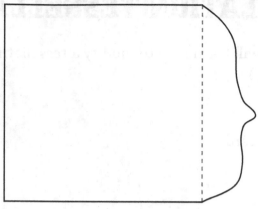

2. If you want your new shape to tessellate, would the bump have to fit into a hole on the opposite side of the square? Why or why not?

★ Now, imagine this. Suppose you cut out a hole in the shape of a bump from one side of the square and moved that section across the square to create a bump on the opposite side of the square. Your new shape would look like this:

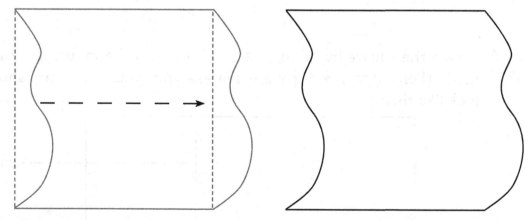

3. Would the new shape tessellate?

★ Try it. Take the square that you cut out and draw a line from one corner of your square, up and around to the other corner of the square, making a bump shape inside the square. It can be any kind of bump or bumps you want. Keep it fairly simple the first time though.

★ Cut the bump shape out and slide the piece across the square and tape it to the opposite side. Like this:

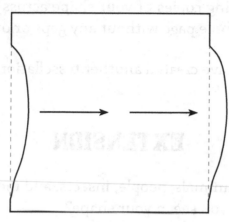

★ Now do the same to the top and bottom of the square. Draw a bump that extends from corner to corner across the bottom of the square. Cut it out. Slide it up and tape it to the top of the square.

Now, you should have something like this:

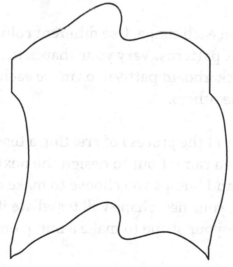

4. Will your new shape tessellate? Why or why not?

★ Take your new shape and place it on a piece of paper.

★ Trace all around the shape and then move it straight over (slide it) and trace around it again. Keep going until you reach the end of the page.

★ Slide the shape up and down, tracing it as you go along. By the time you are finished tracing copies of your shape across the page, you should have filled the whole page without any gaps or overlap.

Congratulations! You have created another tessellation. Does it remind you of anything?

EXTENSION

M. C. Escher made animals, people, insects, and more with his tessellations. What do you see in your shape?

A. Color your shape so that it looks more like what it resembles. Give it eyes, a hat, a fin, an eye, or whatever it needs. Remember that whatever you do, you must do the same thing to each shape.

or

B. Make a pattern on each shape. Use different colors for the same pattern or use different patterns. Vary your shapes in some regular way, like making a checkerboard pattern, or make each shape absolutely different from all of the others.

Now that you understand the process of creating a tessellation by translation rotation, you can set out to design the next shape to look as you wish by the holes and bumps you choose to make on the sides of your shape. Remember that your new shape will tessellate if you always shift the same shape hole across your shape to make a bump on the opposite side.

LESSON 2.7: ROTATIONAL SYMMETRY TESSELLATION

This lesson is based on the same idea as Lesson 2.6, but the activity works by rotating the hole around the shape to make a bump instead of sliding it across.

Materials

* ★ 4" by 6" index card
* ★ ruler
* ★ scissors
* ★ pencil
* ★ multiple colored pencils, crayons, or markers
* ★ tape

Procedure

* ★ Start by making a square again, using an index card.

* ★ Using a ruler, find the middle of one side of your square. Using a pencil, make a little dot there.

* ★ Make a line from the dot to the inside corner of the square. Cut this section out. Then rotate the section around the point so that it is below your dot.

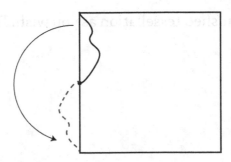

★ Tape the section to the opposite half of the square's side so that it makes a bump.

★ Repeat steps 1–4 for each of the remaining three sides of the square.

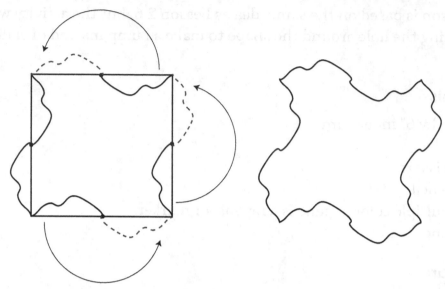

Your new shape will tessellate if you rotate it around the midpoint of its side.

★ Cut out your new shape.

★ Place it on a piece of paper and trace around it.

★ Now, put a pencil point down on the midpoint mark on one side of the new shape and rotate the shape around that point until it fits next to the shape that you just traced without any gaps or overlap. Trace the shape.

★ Do the same thing around the midpoint of each side, tracing your shape as you go along. Your drawing should cover the whole page without leaving any gaps or making any overlaps.

★ Decorate your finished tessellation as you wish. Does this one resemble an object?

LESSON 2.8: TESSELLATION FINAL PROJECT

1. Create two tessellations. One tessellation must use translation symmetry and the other must use rotational symmetry.

2. Decorate both tessellations. You may color them in so that they resemble an object or you may decorate them using creative patterns and colors for each individual shape. Remember that each tessellation must fill a large piece of paper completely.

Extra credit. Use one of the other two tessellating regular polygons besides a square to make one or both of your tessellations. Figure out how to make your regular polygon (triangle or hexagon) tessellate, either by using translation or rotational symmetry.

EXTENSION: TESSELLATION QUILTS

For this lesson, you will create your own tessellating square from fabric. You will then work with your group to assemble your tessellating squares into one, very beautiful tessellation quilt. You may want to ask an adult for help with this project by contributing materials and/or helping with assembly.

Materials

* different kinds of stiff cotton fabric with a wide variety of patterns
* plain white fabric cut into 12" × 12" squares
* backing fabric that is the same size that the quilt is expected to be when complete
* iron-on fusible fabric adhesive
* one iron
* fabric markers
* sewing machine to put all the squares together
* one shape made from an index card during Lesson 2.6 or Lesson 2.7

Procedure

* Pick at least two patterns of fabric that you like.

* Iron the adhesive onto the back of the chosen fabrics.

* Using one of the tessellating shapes that you made from an index card during Lesson 2.6 or Lesson 2.7, lay the shape on the back of the fabric.

* Trace the shape on the piece of fabric in pencil and then cut it out. Remember that it is best not to get *too* detailed in these shapes, as fabric can only hold so much detail. Make sure that you always trace the shape on the back of the fabric, keeping the same side of the card facing up. If you vary the side of the card that you use to trace your shapes, then your shapes will not tessellate.

* Repeat this process with each fabric pattern until you have many different copies of your shape.

* Using iron-on fabric adhesive, glue the tessellating shapes down in their proper positions on the square to create a tessellation, either by

using translation or rotational symmetry. Continue until the entire square of fabric is covered.

★ Sign your name on the square in fabric marker.

★ Ask your teacher or another adult to sew your square onto the quilt.

Quilt created by the students at Varnum Brook Middle School in Pepperell, MA.

THE JOURNEY HOME

Maurits was completely overwhelmed to discover the pictures that he could make once he understood what shapes he had to use to create his tessellating art. He figured out how to make tessellations using both translational and rotational symmetry.

"I couldn't have done it without you two," he said.

"We know," answered Harriet.

"Leonardo felt the same way," said Thomas.

"Leonardo who?"

"da Vinci, of course," answered Harriet, matter-of-factly. "We had to help him with another type of math problem."

"You met Leonardo da Vinci? But how could that be? Didn't he live hundreds of years ago?"

"Yes, but we travel through time. Right now isn't our time either, although it is much closer to our time than Leo's, a mere 97 years ago to be exact."

"97 years ago?"

"Yep," said Harriet. "And let me tell you, your pictures are really popular in our time."

"My pictures," said a confused Maurits, "popular?"

"Don't worry about it," interrupted Thomas. "My sister gets these wacky ideas sometimes. It's best to ignore her at those times."

Thomas glanced at the sky. Dark clouds had begun rolling in.

"I believe we are overstaying our welcome here anyhow," said Thomas as he tapped Harriet on the shoulder and pointed to the sky. "We need to go."

"It's been great knowing you," said Maurits. "Thanks for all of your help! Here, please take this fish picture."

"Thank you!" answered Harriet. Maurits shook the twins' hands and ran off toward the town.

Just as Maurits disappeared into the distance, a crash of thunder shook the ground.

"I think we need to learn to leave before the rain starts," said Harriet, hiding the picture under her sweatshirt. Lightning flashed across the sky. Thomas pulled out his cell phone and twirled the windmill that said home. There was a bang and a flash and then . . .

They were standing outside of the gates of The Dakota again.

"Hey!" said the guard. "What are you kids doing around here all the time?"

"You wouldn't believe us if we told you," answered Harriet.

GLOSSARY

Congruent: Exactly the same.

Equilateral Triangle: A triangle that has all equal sides and angles.

Line Symmetry: The quality of being made up of exactly congruent parts facing each other across a line.

Plane: A flat surface that goes on forever in all directions.

Rotate: To move in a circle around a central point.

Rotational Symmetry: The quality of having exactly congruent parts rotating around an axis.

Symmetry: The quality of being made up of exactly congruent parts facing each other, or around an axis.

Translation: Sliding symmetry.

Two-dimensional: Having only two dimensions, length and width, but no height. Flat.

Vertex: The point of an angle.

UNIT
3

EGYPTIANS AND AREA

They didn't have any machines to use. How did they figure out how to
make the pyramids the right shapes and angles and so on?

—Thomas

TEACHER'S GUIDE

About the Unit

For this unit, students will travel back in time to Ancient Egypt. There
they will meet the Ancient Egyptian architect, Imhotep, who is having trouble designing a pyramid for the Pharaoh Djoser. Students will then follow
along as Harriet and Thomas try to use math to solve Imhotep's problem.

As students work through the lessons in the unit, they will investigate
angles and area. By the time that they finish the unit, students will have a
solid understanding of the surface area of three-dimensional shapes and
they will be able to put their newfound knowledge to practical use by building a mobile with three-dimensional shapes.

Skills

For this last and most challenging section, students will be required
to come up with their own equations for the area of three-dimensional
shapes and will have to reason out the answers for themselves, making

some pretty large leaps in their thinking. In order to complete this section, they will need to use many of the skills that they learned in the last two units.

In addition, students must be able to multiply large numbers and understand the concept of equations.

About the Lessons

Lesson 3.1: Making a Perfect Square. For this lesson, students will look at how a square can be created without using the modern tools that we take for granted. This process will force them to consider new aspects of figures, such as equality of length and angles. As students work through the lesson, they will also revisit the idea of ratio from Unit 1.

Lesson 3.2: Making the Pyramid Face the Right Way. For this lesson, students will use their understanding of angles once again, this time by using the rising of the sun to find north.

Lesson 3.3: Area of Rectangles. For this lesson, students will use what they know to come up with the equation for the area of a rectangle.

Lesson 3.4: Area of Triangles. For this lesson, students will take their figuring further by coming up with the equation for the area of a triangle.

Lesson 3.5: Surface Area of Three-Dimensional Shapes. For this lesson, students will combine the area equations that they have come up with in their previous lessons to find out the surface area of three-dimensional shapes.

Lesson 3.6: Cylinder Extra Challenge. This lesson is designed for your students who need an extra challenge. It will require them to work with pi and decimals and to take apart a cylinder in their minds. Allow students to use 3.14 for pi and a calculator if you wish.

Extension. For the final project in this unit, students will make a mobile with different three-dimensional shapes that all have the same surface area. Students may not be able to *make* the shapes exactly to measurement, but they should be able to describe them exactly. They will need to figure out how to do this on their own.

Students can work alone, completing the lesson at home for a project, or they may work in pairs or in groups in class. A structured example may be offered to students for writing their explanation if the teacher thinks it is required. (See p. 132 for a structured example.)

You may want the student to figure out how to put what they do into words themselves. It is even more challenging that way. Suggest that students explain what they did verbally to someone else before they try to write it down.

Note: Teachers are asked to help math students of all abilities learn to explain *how* they do the problem, as well as get the right answer. This can be quite a challenge to gifted math students, who often "just know" it is right. See the answer key on page 132 of Appendix B for a structured example of what a student should say.

THE THIRD ADVENTURE

For several weeks after they returned home from 20th-century Holland, Harriet and Thomas didn't even try going to The Dakota. They didn't really wonder about much either. Instead, they spent hours at home making their own tessellation quilt.

The twins kept themselves busy for the next several weeks by cutting out shapes in different fabrics and putting the squares together until they had a 6 × 4 foot beautiful patterned quilt to hang on the wall. Once they were finished with the quilt, they tried to figure out the correct ratios for parts of all kinds of weird objects—from a flashlight to a computer. The twins also spent time outside in Central Park and took the subway to the beach in Brooklyn where they could just enjoy the summertime.

One day, it was chilly outside and Thomas noticed that some of the leaves on the maple tree outside of their building had a reddish tinge.

"Fall is coming," he sighed, as he wrapped his arms around his chest, "and that means school."

The twins liked school. They were in the same class most years and they enjoyed learning new information and seeing their friends again after the long summer. But the end of summer vacation with all of its freedom and exciting experiences was always sad.

"We need one last adventure before we end it all and go back to school," said Harriet.

"But this time," said Thomas, "I want to travel to somewhere way, way in the past."

"And I want to go somewhere warm," Harriet shivered.

"We could travel to the time of the dinosaurs in Africa," suggested Thomas.

"That would be great," replied Harriet, "but what kind of question or problem involving mathematics existed back then?"

"How many dinosaurs can fit into a small cave?" asked Thomas.

"Just who would we be helping?"

"The cleverest dinosaur," said Thomas.

"How about Ancient Greece? There is the ancient mathematician **Pythagoras**. I bet he had some great things to wonder about," said Harriet.

"Wait, I know where we can go!" said Thomas. He put one hand in front of his face high up in the air and one hand lower down behind his back, with each hand making a sharp angle at the wrist. He turned his head to the side and began walking in a weird way, sliding the hands back and forth at the same time.

"What are you doing?" asked Harriet.

"Walking like an Egyptian," answered Thomas. "The Ancient Egyptians have always been my favorites. You know, King Tut, and all that."

That would be great! We could see the pyramids when they were new," said Harriet.

"And the Sphinx being carved," said Thomas.

"But who would we help there? I mean, was there even any math being done way back then?" asked Harriet.

"I don't think so," said Thomas, disappointed. "And anyway, how would we know about it if there was?"

"We could try the library," suggested Harriet.

"Now, there's an idea!" replied Thomas as he pulled a silver library access card out of his pocket.

The twins set out for the New York Public Library's main Humanities branch on 5th Avenue and 42nd Street. It was another one of their favorite buildings. As they approached the library, Harriet waved at the two stone lions sitting out front. She wondered if they ever came alive in the same way that the gargoyle and the dragons did at The Dakota. Inside the library, the tall marble columns, the beautiful painted ceilings of mythic figures, and the long tables filled with quiet banks of people reading gave her the usual feeling of calm.

They went up to the research librarian, who was always helpful

in their searches for information, no matter what subject they wanted to know about this time.

The twins told her that they wanted to find out if mathematics was used in ancient Egypt. She asked them if they knew about the Rhind Mathematical Papyrus. They knew nothing about it.

"It was a series of math problems written by a scribe in ancient Egypt," she said.

"That sounds like the right kind of thing," said Harriet.

The librarian wrote down the name of a book called *Ancient Egypt, Math, and Architecture* on a call slip and instructed the twins to drop the slip off at one of the long oak desks in the Rose Reading Room.

Then, once their number was called, Harriet and Thomas could pick up their book.

Inside the book, the twins found a number of pictures of the Rhind Mathematical Papyrus. Some of the problems on the papyrus were translated into English.

"This is so cool!" said Thomas. He turned some more pages and came upon a picture of the Great Pyramid of Giza.

"I wonder how in the world they managed to build those huge things," sighed Harriet.

"They didn't have any machines to use," replied Thomas. "How did they figure out how to make the pyramids the right shapes and angles and so on?"

"It says here that most of that pyramid and many others were designed by an architect called Imhotep," said Harriet.

"You mean one person figured all that out?" said Thomas. "I bet he could have used our help to do that!"

Harriet met his eyes. "I bet you're right," she said. "I wonder how anyone could have figured all that out."

Thomas made sure that he had his phone and then, grabbing Harriet's hand, began running uptown toward The Dakota. Now that they were trying to go to Ancient Egypt, he seemed to have forgotten all about his wariness of danger.

Sure enough, when they had snuck as usual past the guard, they found that the stairs had appeared again at the foot of the gargoyle.

For once, Thomas led the way as they climbed as fast as they could up the tiny stone steps. The gargoyle seemed to be expecting them this time. He acted like an old friend, smiling at the twins affectionately. The dragons even turned their heads away so that their fire would not burn them.

"Go on," the gargoyle said.

Thomas took Harriet's hand and, without pausing, grabbed hold of the gargoyle's beard.

"I wonder how Imhotep ever built those pyramids," he said. There was a flash of light, a banging sound, and then . . .

The twins looked around. The twins were surrounded by blue-white sky and sand and not a single person was in sight. Instead, there was just sand and more sand as far as the eye could see. Thomas wiped his forehead with his palm.

It was a blazing hot midday. The sun was right over their heads and it was hotter than any sun they had ever felt before.

Harriet began fanning herself with her hands while Thomas pulled out his phone. The phone was made of sandstone now, with **hieroglyphic**-labeled keys.

The twins looked around and began walking toward a tall dune in front of them. In the distance, behind the dune, they could just barely see the outline of a group of small tents. Thomas and Harriet looked at each other, nodded, and began to walk toward the tents.

As they approached, a young man came out of one of the tents and stood looking down at the flat sand in front of him. He was a dark-haired man wearing a white linen kilt and he had a worried expression on his face. Harriet and Thomas looked at each other. At the same time, they both said "Imhotep." The young man looked up.

He spoke. Of course, they couldn't understand him at all.

Thomas pushed the button on his phone that looked like a picture of person's ear with a hand cupping it . . . and his words became clear. " . . . design the perfect pyramid for the Pharaoh Djoser, may his reign be long. I said that I would do it, of course, because I must do all that the Pharaoh commands, but I am not sure that I can. There are so many problems I don't know how to solve."

"Like what?" asked Harriet.

"Well, the pyramid must be perfectly square, and it must face in the right direction. And I must order of all the right amounts of surface stone ahead of time without seeing the finished pyramid."

"Perhaps we can help you," said Thomas. "We are pretty good at helping people. I'm Thomas, and this is my sister, Harriet."

"If you would help me, I would be forever grateful to you both and I would make sure that you have a tomb of great beauty prepared for you."

"Um, thanks," said Harriet, "but we would just do it for fun."

"For fun?" said Imhotep, as though he had never thought of doing anything for that reason.

"Just tell us the details of your first problem," said Harriet.

LESSON 3.1:
MAKING A PERFECT SQUARE

Imhotep told the twins that the square was a very important shape to the Egyptians. It carried a deep religious significance. So his pyramid must be a perfect square.

Imhotep wanted to mark off the square base in the sand for the builders to use. He had a length of rope measured off into 12 equal parts. At the end of each section, he had made a knot. The distance between the knots was one **royal cubit**. (A royal cubit was the Egyptian unit of measurement that equaled about 20.5 inches.)

Imhotep knew that he could make sure that all of the sides of the pyramid were the same length. He showed Harriet how to make a four-sided figure with all of the sides of equal length using the rope. "I can hammer a spike into the sand, tie the end of my rope to it, count four knots, put in another spike, count four knots and keep going around the spikes, making sure that there are four knots on each of the four sides."

This is what Imhotep had:

"If I used a much longer rope, I could make a huge shape with four equal sides. It would be big enough for the base of the pyramid."

"So, you're all set," said Thomas.

"But my shape would not be a square!" said Imhotep.

1. Imhotep is correct. Why isn't the shape he could make a square?

2. ***Abstract Thinking Question.*** What ideas do you have for how Imhotep might fix his problem? Remember that he only has the rope and some stakes with which to measure and make his shape.

Harriet saw immediately that Imhotep's shape was not a **square**. Even though the lengths of the sides were all equal, the angles were not. To make the shape a square, the angles all had to be equal as well. She remembered from their work with Maurits Escher that each of the angles of a square must be 90 degrees.

"Without those 90 degree angles, your pyramid won't be a perfect square," she told Imhotep.

"I know," sighed Imhotep. "What shall I do?"

Harriet had an idea. She knew that a 90-degree angle, the kind of corner angle that Imhotep needed for his square, was called a **right angle**. This is the symbol for a right angle:

Harriet also remembered certain mathematical rules about triangles with right angles that she thought might help the twins solve Imhotep's problem.

"The first thing we need to remember," Harriet noted, "is that a **right triangle** is a triangle with a right angle in it."

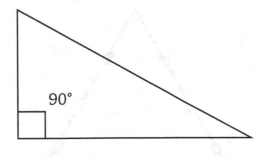

90°

3. Can a triangle have more than one right angle in it? Why or why not?

"And," Harriet continued, "you always have a right triangle if the measurement of the sides of your triangle is 3", 4", and 5" or any 3 numbers in the same ratio to each other."

4. Take a piece of string and see if Harriet is correct. You can use inches instead of cubits as long as the ratio stays the same. The ratio must be 3:4:5.

Materials

* ★ piece of string
* ★ scissors
* ★ ruler
* ★ black marker

Procedure

* ★ Measure a piece of string 12 inches long.
* ★ Cut it.
* ★ Take a black marker and a ruler and make a mark on the string at every one-inch measure.
* ★ Now make a triangle with your string.

Remember that there is more than one kind of triangle you can make with this string. Here is one:

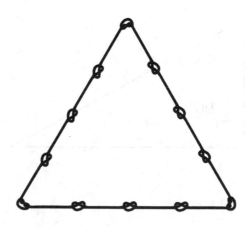

5. Make a different triangle with the string, and then draw it below. Make two other triangles. Draw them. Make sure that you put the black knot marks in your drawing.

6. Make a triangle with your string that has 3 inches on one side, 4 on the second side and 5 on the third. In fact, if you make one side 3 inches, and another side 3 inches, the last side will be have to be 5 inches. Draw it.

7. If Harriet is correct, this triangle must be a right triangle. Is it a right triangle?

8. Is there any way to make a triangle with these measurements that is not a right triangle?

   If so, draw it.

9. If a triangle had the sides 6", 8", and 10", would it also be a right triangle?

10. How about if the triangle's sides were 60", 80", and 100"? Would that one be a right triangle also?

11. Now that you know how to make a right triangle with rope, how could you use this knowledge to make a square using only string marked in 12 equal sections? Write and draw your answer.

12. How can Imhotep stake out his square for the base of the pyramid he wants to build? Use cartoons/or stick figures of the ancient Egyptians, words, and your idea from Problem 10 to describe how you would use a long rope to stake out the square base of the pyramid. Number the steps that you would use. The first step has been done for you.

Step 1: The Egyptians would make a very long rope with 12 evenly spaced knots.

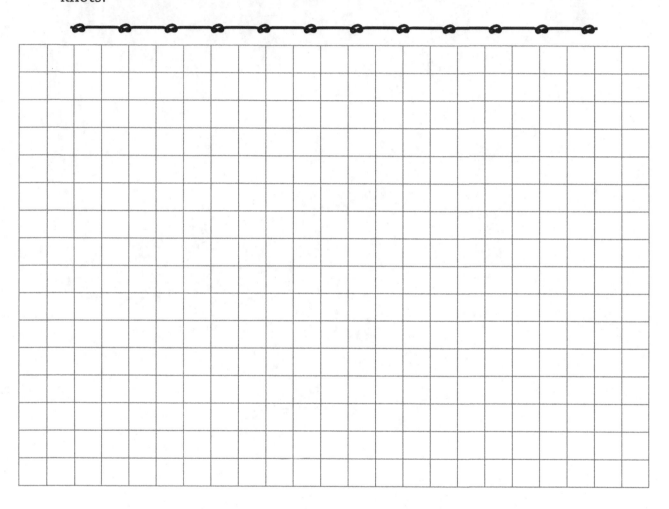

LESSON 3.2: MAKING THE PYRAMID FACE THE RIGHT WAY

Once he knew how to make a perfect square, Imhotep confronted another challenge. "A true pyramid must face in the correct direction," he said.

"One side must face due north, and the other side due south. So, before we can draw out the base, we must figure out what direction is due north." He peered out over the sand at the rising sun.

"That should be easy," Thomas said. "Just use a compass."

"A what?" asked Imhotep.

"You know," said Thomas. "One of those little round things that has the arrow that always points due north." Imhotep looked at Thomas as if he had lost his mind.

"Like this," Thomas drew a compass in the sand. "Magnets make it work."

"What kind of nets?" Imhotep looked even more confused.

"MAGNETS," yelled Thomas, as if speaking more loudly would make his ideas clearer.

"Thomas," Harriet tapped her brother lightly on the shoulder.

"M. A. G. N. E . . . " Thomas was spelling it out.

"Thomas, when was the compass invented?" Harriet asked quietly.

"Oh yeah," said Thomas, "not for another 2,300 years or so."

"And I think that was in China. The idea took another 1,000 years or so years to get to this area."

"Well, you don't happen to have one in your pocket, do you?" asked Thomas.

Imhotep was looking at the two of them curiously.

"No," said Harriet. "Anyway, what would it do to history if we introduced the compass now? That might change the course of civilization!"

Imhotep walked away from them. He seemed lost in thought and was staring straight up at the sun.

"Hey, don't stare at the sun," Harriet called to Imhotep. "It's bad for your eyes."

"If only the sun came up in the north, we could face the side of the pyramid towards its rising point," said Imhotep. "But it rises in the east and sets in the west, so that's no good."

"I guess at least they already know at this time where the sun rises and sets," said Thomas. "How can we use this knowledge to help Imhotep find exact north?"

"I don't know," replied Harriet.

"Eureka!" shouted Thomas.

"Is that Greek?" asked Imhotep.

"I know how we can find north and south by using angles again!" said Thomas.

1. **Abstract Thinking Question.** How can Imhotep find exact north and south using angles?

Thomas suggested that they start by putting a tall stick in the ground. Then, they should draw a circle around the stick by tying a rock to the end of a rope the same length as the stick, and dragging it all the way around the stick so that it makes a circle in the sand.

Thomas said, "Now, if we stand by the stick first thing in the morning when the sun is coming up, we can mark exactly where our shadow falls on the circle."

"But that direction where the shadow falls is not north or south!" said Harriet. "That's east, because the sun is coming up there."

2. Harriet made a mistake about what direction the sun will cast a shadow in the morning. What was her mistake?

"Then we can do the same thing at the end of the day and see where the setting sun makes a mark on the circle," said Thomas.

3. What direction will that evening shadow mark show?

"But neither one of those will tell us north or south," said Harriet.

"No," said Imhotep, "They will just tell us east and west. But at least that's a start."

The three did exactly what Thomas had suggested. Draw the stick and the circle made out of rope in the space below.

4. How do you think Harriet and Thomas and Imhotep could take the next step and find north and south? Draw and write your answer.

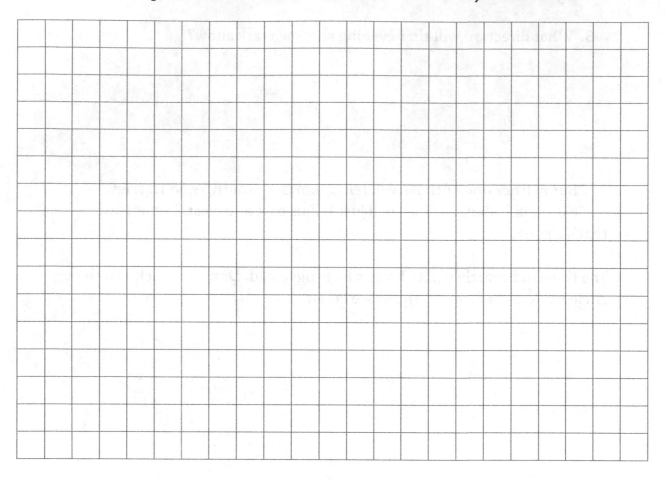

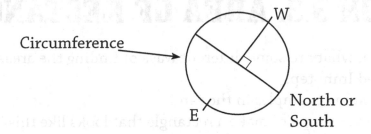

Circumference — North or South

"Here's what you do," Thomas suggested. "Measure halfway across the middle (the **diameter**) of the circle and make a right angle there with one side touching the mark at the east. Then use the rope method we figured out before to make the right angle. At a right angle to that will be north or south."

"That's great!" said Imhotep. "Now I know how to face the pyramid north and south, and how to make sure that it is a perfect square. Thank you both so much!"

Harriet and Thomas looked as modest as they could.

"I have just one other problem," he said. "When we finish building our pyramid steps out of limestone, we will have to use marble casing to smooth the surface. How much of the special white marble shall I order, and have brought up the river on barges? I have to send the men out to get the stone months in advance because it takes so long for the workers to dig the marble up out of the quarries and then put it on rafts and send it up the Nile to the building site. How can I figure out in advance how much stone I will need?" he worried. "If I order too much, it will be a waste of time and money, but if I order too little, I won't be able to finish the pyramid! The Pharaoh will get very grouchy with me if his burial place isn't finished when I promised. He will be afraid that he will die and have no place ready to be buried. A Pharaoh must be buried within 10 days of his death."

"An angry Pharaoh is not a good thing," agreed Thomas.

"What do you know about the measurements of the outside of a pyramid?" asked Harriet.

"Well," said Imhotep, "the outside area measurement would be equal to all of the outside, flat shapes put together."

"What shapes are on the outside surface of a pyramid?" asked Thomas.

"There are triangles," said Harriet. "Four of them."

"And a square base," said Imhotep. "We don't have to cover the base with marble, but we should know its area so that we know how many stone base blocks we need to get."

"So, there are four triangles and one square," said Thomas.

"There are ways to figure out the area of certain shapes," offered Harriet.

"Yes! There are rules with numbers that always work," replied Thomas.

LESSON 3.3: AREA OF RECTANGLES

"Well, then, what are some different ways of finding the areas of shapes?" asked Imhotep.

Thomas drew some examples in the sand.

"If you use your rope to make a rectangle that looks like this:"

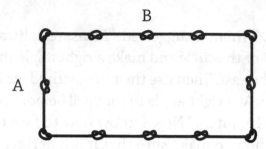

1. What is the length of side A of this rectangle? (Remember, the distance between the knots is a royal cubit.)

2. What is the length of side B of this rectangle?

3. If you draw lines between the knots to make squares inside the rectangle, what is the area, in squares, of this shape? (Area is written in square units, such as square inches or centimeters. In this case, they are square cubits.)

"If you use a longer rope, you can make this," Thomas drew this rectangle in the sand.

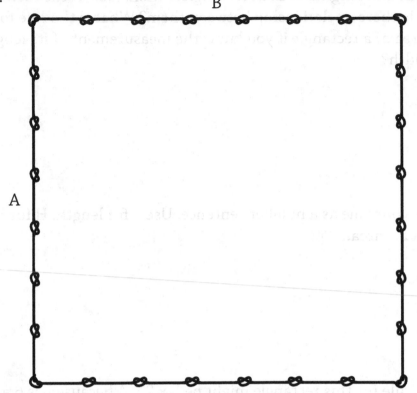

4. What is the length of side A of this rectangle?

5. What is the length of side B of this rectangle?

6. What is the area of this rectangle?

7. **Abstract Thinking Question.** Look at the measurements for the lengths and heights of both rectangles. Then, look at the rectangles' area. Is there a relationship between them? What is the rule for finding the area of a rectangle if you know the measurement of its length and its width?

8. Write your rule as a number sentence. Use L for length, H for height, and A for area.

A possible rule for this rectangle might be L × 2 = A because L is 6 and 6 × 2 does equal 12, the area.

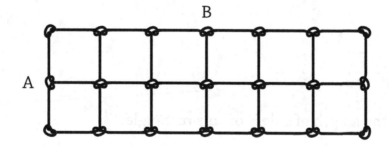

9. Is the above rule true for *all* rectangles? Does the length times two always equal the area? Why or why not?

10. What is a rule that is always true for the area of all rectangles, written as a number sentence? (Remember, L is length, H is height and A is area. The = sign denotes equals. A number sentence with an equal sign in it is called an equation.)

11. Is there a different rule for the area of a square that will not work for other rectangles? What is an area equation for squares only?

LESSON 3.4: AREA OF TRIANGLES

"So now we can find the area of the square at the base of the pyramid as long as we know the length of its sides," said Imhotep, "But what about the four triangles that are the rest of its surface?"

"Well, if you draw a diagonal line down the center of a rectangle, making it into two triangles, what is the area of each of these triangles?" replied Harriet.

1. What is the answer to Harriet's question?

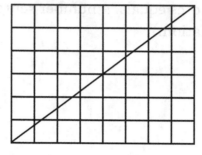

2. What is the equation for the area of triangles? Use H for height, L for length, and A for area again. Use the = sign.

3. Is this equation always true for all triangles?

4. Are all triangles half of some rectangle or square?

Draw several triangles below. Draw the rectangles or squares as well.

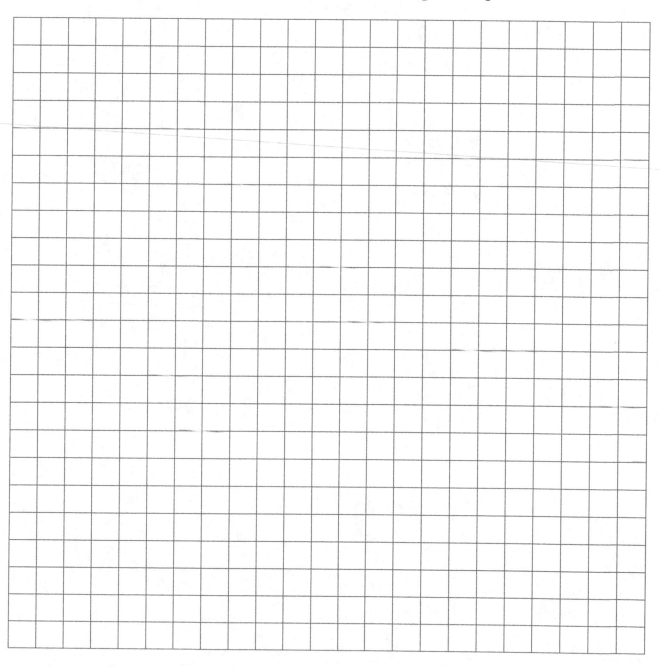

5. Does your equation for area of triangles hold true for *all* triangles? Remember to use the height (H), which is not always the same length as a side of the triangle.

LESSON 3.5: SURFACE AREA OF THREE-DIMENSIONAL SHAPES

"Now that we know how to figure out the surface of the pyramid . . ." began Harriet.

"We need to put all of our equations together and fill in the real amounts," interrupted Imhotep. "Then we can figure out the surface area of **three-dimensional** shapes."

"What would the formula be for the entire surface area of the whole pyramid, including the base?" asked Thomas.

1. "Break it down into parts," said Harriet. "First the square base. What is the formula for the area of the square?"

2. "Then the triangles," said Thomas. "Their equations are . . ."

"And there are four of them, don't forget," said Imhotep.

3. So the equation for the surface area of the *whole* pyramid, including all its parts would be:

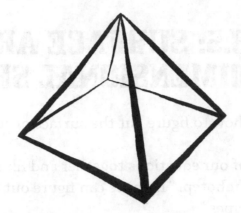

In the problems below are the approximate measurements of the Great Pyramid of Giza (which Imhotep designed for the Pharaoh Khufu). The measurements are in cubits. This unit of measurement came from the length of a person's forearm (the distance from the thumb to the elbow). The Egyptian hieroglyph for the cubit was an arm.

4. The Egyptian cubit was not divided into centimeters, or inches, but into palms and digits. The cubit was divided into 7 "palms" of 4 "digits," making _____ parts in all.

Each side of the square base of the pyramid at Giza was 440 cubits long. The height of each of the triangles on its four sides was 356 cubits.

5. What was the area Imhotep had to cover with the white marble? Show your work. Remember to use square cubits as your unit for area.

6. What was the area of the base of the pyramid?

7. What was the area of the whole surface of the great pyramid at Giza?

8. If all of the angles in the three-dimensional shape below are right angles, then what is the surface area of this shape? Show the area for each part and how you found the total area.

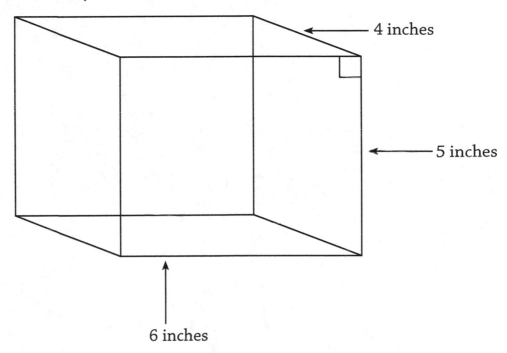

4 inches

5 inches

6 inches

9. What is the surface area of this prism? Remember to think about what shapes you would have if you took this prism apart. Show all parts of your calculations.

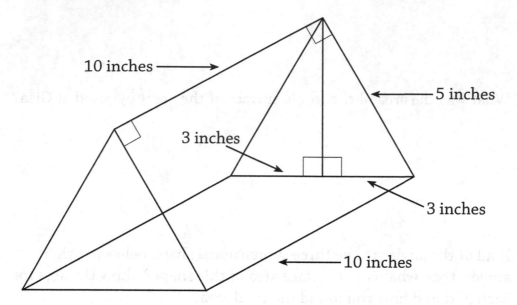

LESSON 3.6: CYLINDER EXTRA CHALLENGE

There is evidence that the Ancient Egyptians were aware of **pi**. Strangely, the length of any side of the Giza Pyramid base, times two, divided by its height is equal to 3.14 (pi). Did Imhotep do this for a reason?

The area of a circle is always equal to the **radius,** multiplied by itself, times the number **pi.** The **radius** is the distance from the center of a circle to its edge.

Pi is a special number that is in many equations involving circles. We can use **3.14** to estimate pi, although in reality pi goes on for many, many decimal places (**3.14159265 . . .** and so on).

The distance around any circle (the **circumference** of that circle) is equal to 2 times the radius, times pi.

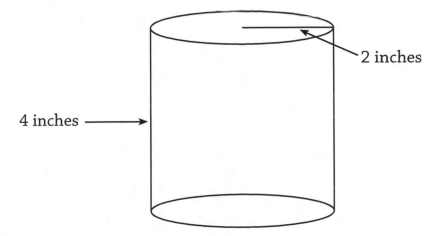

2 inches

4 inches

What is the surface area of this cylinder? Remember to think about what shapes you would have if you took the cylinder apart.

Show the area for each part and how you can find the total area. The radius of each circle is 2 inches. The height of the cylinder is 4 inches.

1. The area of each end shape is:

2. The area of the side of the cylinder is:

3. The surface area of the cylinder is:

EXTENSION

Create a mobile (a hanging, balanced sculpture) made out of paper that has at least three different, **three-dimensional** shapes. They must either:

★ All have the same surface area so that they will be balanced, or

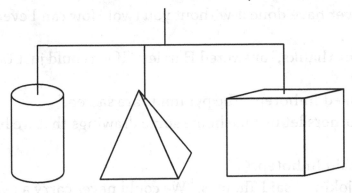

★ One shape can equal the surface area of the other two put together, so that they will balance like this:

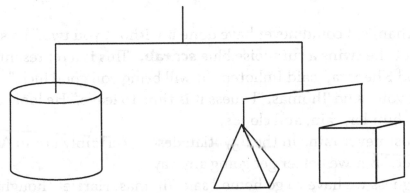

Rules for the Challenge

★ You may use any three-dimensional regular shapes you like as long as no two shapes are exactly the same shape and size.

★ Your model should be made out of paper, tape, and string. It does not have to be perfect, but the math you use should be correct.

★ You must explain, in mathematical language using words, pictures and equations, what shapes you used and the way you figured out each shape's surface area. Turn this in with your mobile in a typed, or hand-written finished paragraph version. The writing is at least as important as the mobile.

THE END OF THE ADVENTURE

Imhotep was ready to begin building his pyramid. He had staked out the **square** shape for the base and had made sure it faced the right way, and he had ordered the stone for the building.

"I could never have done it without you two! How can I ever thank you?" he asked.

"No need for thanks," answered Harriet. "If we could just take home a small pyramid . . . "

"What?" asked Imhotep. "The pyramids are sacred."

"Well, the others let us take home some drawings that we helped with," said Harriet.

"Others?" said Imhotep.

"She's just joking," said Thomas. "We could never carry a pyramid home anyway."

"Joking?" said Imhotep. Harriet wondered if humor had been invented yet.

"Well, thanks, I could never have done it without you two," he said. He gave each of the twins a turquoise blue **scarab.** "This is a representation of the sun god Khepera," said Imhotep. "It will bring you good luck."

"Thank you," said Thomas. "I guess it is time to leave." He looked around, expecting thunder, rain, and clouds.

"It almost never rains in the Egyptian desert, certainly not in August," said Harriet. "But we better get going anyway."

"Yes, I guess we have to go home," said Thomas. Harriet thought he looked quite sad.

"I hate to leave too," she said. "It's been so much fun in Egypt. I wish we could see the pyramids finished."

"Come back when they're done," said Imhotep. "It will only take a few dozen years." He bowed his goodbye.

"How do you get home from here?" he asked.

"Well," said Harriet.

"It just kind of happens," said Thomas. The twins reached out and grasped each other's hands. Thomas pulled out his phone. The button for home showed a palace.

"Goodbye," they bowed back. A great sand cloud blew up suddenly off the nearest dune. The twins had to cover their eyes with their arms to keep the sand out. Sand stung their skin and blew into their hair. It was difficult to breathe. Then, suddenly, all was quiet.

When the twins opened their eyes, they were back at The Dakota. The guard spotted them immediately and he was definitely angry this time.

"Now see here, you kids, you can't just be hanging around like this. Move along now," he said. "There is nothing to see here."

"That's what you think," said Thomas.

"I guess we won't be able to get back inside there for a while," said Harriet.

She thought she heard strange laughter coming from the top of the building. It was a rough, low-pitched laughter. It sounded like it was coming from a throat made out of rock.

"Listen to that," said Thomas. "He's laughing." They looked up toward the top corner of the building where the gargoyle lived.

"Goodbye! See you next summer!" echoed the voice.

The twins looked at each other and smiled. They walked home together through the cool fall day.

GLOSSARY

Circumference: The distance around a circle.

Diameter: The distance across the center of a circle.

Diagonal: A line going across a shape from corner to corner.

Hieroglyphics: A written language using pictures to represent sounds, words, or syllables.

Right Angle: An angle measuring 90 degrees. The symbol for a right angle is: ⌐

Right Triangle: A triangle with a right angle in it.

Pi: A number that occurs in many parts of the measurement of a circle (e.g., the area of a circle equals pi times the radius squared). Pi is often approximated by 3.14, but is actually a much longer decimal.

Radius: Half of the diameter, from the central point of a circle to its edge.

Square: A rectangle having all equal length sides.

Three-dimensional: Having length, width, and height.

APPENDIX
A

HOW TO MAKE
A FABRIC
TESSELLATION QUILT

For this project, each student will create his or her own tessellating square from fabric. Then, all of the squares will be assembled together into a tessellation quilt.

Created by the students at Varnum Brook Middle School in Pepperell, MA.

These quilts are very beautiful when made out of real fabric. In order to participate in this project, children must be old enough to handle sharp scissors. Parents can help by contributing materials for the project, or, if they have time, by assisting students with assembly. If you are doing this project with a large group, a parent volunteer can be very helpful in the classroom by helping you iron and cut the fabric.

Materials

* different kinds of stiff cotton fabric with a wide variety of patterns
* plain white fabric cut into 12" × 12" squares
* backing fabric that is the same size that the quilt is expected to be when complete
* iron-on fusible fabric adhesive
* one iron
* fabric markers
* sewing machine to put all the squares together.

Procedure

* Ask students to pick at least two patterns of fabric that they like. They will then iron the adhesive on the back of the chosen fabrics. They may use the iron themselves if they are old enough, or they may ask an adult for help.
* Using tessellating shapes made from index cards, have students lay the tessellated card on the fabric, and trace the shape upon it in pencil. Then have students cut it out. Remind students that it is best not to get too detailed in these shapes as fabric can only hold so much detail.
* Ask the students to repeat this process with each fabric pattern they have chosen until they have many different copies of their shape. Make sure that students keep the same side of the card pattern up, or the shape will not tessellate.
* Using iron-on fusible fabric adhesive, have students glue the tessellating shapes down in their proper positions on the white squares in order to create a tessellation using translation or rotational symmetry.
* Ask students to continue until the entire square is covered.
* Once students are finished with their square, ask them to sign their name on the square in fabric marker.
* Sew the squares together so that they form a quilt. If you are skilled enough, you can make a border and backing for the quilt and create

even loops in order to hang it on a rod. If not, you may just put the squares together, hem the edges and still attain a beautiful result.

These wonderful quilts can go on display in the halls of your school or in your classroom. They can then stay there for years as they introduce other students to the idea of tessellations.

Resources

The following website contains several helpful links to other tessellation sites: http://www.tessellations.org/links.htm

Possible Adaptations

* A less labor intensive, paper version of the tessellation quilt can be made by taking the best results from Lesson 2.7, making each tessellation into a paper square, and putting the squares together on a large background paper.
* Alternatively, tessellation squares may be formed by laying tessellating shapes over magazine pictures, tracing around the forms and cutting them out, then tessellating the resulting patterned shapes on a separate sheet of white paper.
* Each student may contribute a square to the final paper quilt.

APPENDIX
B

ANSWER KEY

UNIT 1

Lesson 1.1: Ratio

1. There are many possible answers. A student's answers may include time, money, and age, to name a few.
2. Relationships about friendliness, beauty, or hunger are a few that cannot be represented by numbers, and are therefore not ratios.
3. Yes
4. 150 lbs
5. Multiplication
6. Samantha and Susan have a 2:1 strength ratio, so you know that in order to get Samantha's number, you must multiply Susan's number by 2.
7. Size 8
8. If you knew that the ratio was 1:4 and that Bob wore a size 8, you would make a fraction of the ratio ¼, and make an equation using the known number in a new fraction, this time for the denominator: ¼ = ⅜. You would divide 8 by 4, getting 2 and then multiply 2 times the known numerator, 1: ¼ = ⅜. Then you would turn it back into a ratio 2:8. Norman's shoe size would be 2.
9. Equa is the root word of equation (from Latin, aequus).

Lesson 1.2: Measuring Body Parts

Leonardo and the twins discovered that:	How might you draw it?	How could you write it as a number sentence using letters as symbols?	Test it out on yourself or with a partner. Is it true?	Ratio between parts
1. If a person spreads out his or her arms, the distance from the end of one hand to the end of the other will be equal to that person's height.		H = height A = outspread arms H = A	Yes, it is true! My arms together are 5'1" inch long, and that is my exact height!	1:1
2. The length of the foot from the end of the toes to the heel goes twice into the distance from the heel to the knee.		F = Foot L = Leg 2 × F = L	It was true for my friend, but not for me.	2:1
3. From the tip of the longest finger of the hand to the shoulder joint equals four hands.		H = hands A= arm from end of longest finger to shoulder 4 × H = A	Yes, it was true for both people.	1:4
4. From the tip of the longest finger of the hand to the shoulder joint equals four faces.		A = arm from end of longest finger to shoulder F = face 4 × F = A	No, this was not true for either person.	1:4
5. The thinnest part of the leg in profile goes five times into the distance from the sole of the foot to the knee joint.		LT = leg thickness at thinnest point L = leg, foot to knee 5 × LT = L	It was true for my friend, but not for me.	5:1

Leonardo and the twins discovered that:	How might you draw it?	How could you write it as a number sentence using letters as symbols?	Test it out on yourself or with a partner. Is it true?	Ratio between parts
6. When kneeling, a person loses one fourth of his height.		L = leg from heel to knee H = height $4 \times L = H$	Yes, it was true for both of us.	1:4

Note. The answers in the "test it out" column are sample answers.

2. A student's answers may include: people have different body proportions; they are different ages or gender.
3. A student's answers may include age and/or gender.

Lesson 1.3: Averages

1. You multiply the number of feet by 12 and add the number of inches to the answer.
2. 56"
3. 56"
4. They are equal: 1:1
5.

	Average
height	56"
arm span	56"
foot length	7"
heel to knee	14"
hand	6"
finger to shoulder	24"
face	6"
leg width	3"

6.

Leonardo and the twins discovered that:	Ratio	Is this statement true for the average person in Leonardo's town? Show your work.
If a person spreads out his or her arms, the distance from the end of one hand to the end of the other will be equal to that person's height.	A = arm span H = height A = H	Yes, because 56" = 56".
The length of the foot from the end of the toes to the heel goes twice into the distance from the heel to the knee.	F = foot length K = knee to heel 2:1 = F:K	Yes, because 7" × 2 = 14".
From the tip of the longest finger of the hand to the shoulder joint equals four hands.	A = arm from fingers to shoulder H = hands 1:4 = H:A	Yes, because 4" × 6 = 24".
From the tip of the longest finger of the hand to the shoulder joint equals four faces.	F = faces A = arm from fingers to shoulder 1:4 = F:A	Yes, because 4 × 6" = 24".
The thinnest part of the leg in profile goes five times into the distance from the sole of the foot to the knee joint.	K = knee to heel L = leg width 1:5 = L:K	No, because 3" × 5 does not equal 14"; it equals 15". However, it is close.
When kneeling down, a person loses one fourth of his height.	K = knee to heel H = height 1:4 = K:H	Yes, because 4 × 14 = 56.

7. Many possible answers: not a big enough sample; we rounded the numbers.

8. Closer because the larger number of people measured would lead to a greater statistical likelihood that the group's average measurements fit the rules.

9. This answer depends on your class.

Lesson 1.4: More Ratios

1. There are a few ways this can be done. Here is one example of a student's answer:

Steps: First, I would measure Leonardo's drawing of Maria on page 25. I would find that Maria is 5" tall. I know that Harriet is 5' tall and her desk is 3' tall. Knowing that Harriet's desk must be the same ratio to her height as Maria's desk is to her height, I would figure out this ratio, make it into a fraction, and then multiply the fraction times Maria's height.

2. Maria is 5" tall. Harriet is 5' tall. Harriet's desk is 3' tall. 5' in Harriet's world = 5" in Maria's world. Because one foot equals 12", the ratio is 1:12, or $\frac{1}{12}$. If the desk is 3' tall or 36" in Harriet's world, it would be 3" in Maria's world, because 36 ÷ 12 = 3.
   Answer: Maria's desk height would be 3".

Extension

1. Check width and length of desk against a real desk in your room.
2. Check ratio and actual measurements.

Lesson 1.5: The Giant Hand

1. Again, there are a couple of ways students can do this. Here is one example:
   Steps:
   1. First, I will figure out the ratio between a foot length and height, using my averages from the chart. An average foot is 7" long; average height is 56 inches: 7:56, or $\frac{7}{56}$. I know that 7 × 8 = 56, so the ratio of foot length to height is 1:8.
   2. I know the giant's foot is 14' long, so if I convert that into inches, 14 × 12 = 168" long.
   3. The ratio is 1:8, so I can multiply his foot length by 8, which equals 1,344" tall.
   4. I can turn that back into feet by dividing by 12.

2. The giant is 112' tall.

Lesson 1.6: Drawing Proportions

1. Check to see if student kept the proportions the same in his or her drawing.

Lesson 1.7: Making a Giant Object Group Project

See Rubric on page 134 (Appendix C).

Extra Challenge: Draw a Model of Your Classroom

See Rubric on page 135 (Appendix C).

UNIT 2

Lesson 2.1: Symmetry

1. There are several right answers. Here is one student's answer: Line symmetry is the quality of being made up of exactly identical parts facing each other across a line.

2.

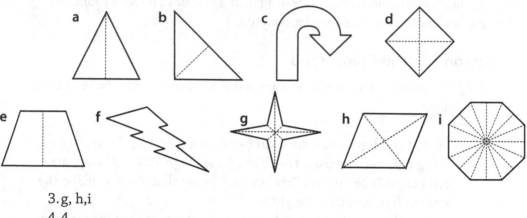

3. g, h, i

4. 4

5. 1

6. 90 degrees

7. Many possible answers: 90 degrees is the same as 15 minutes, each minute is the same as 6 degrees.

8. 90 degrees, 270 degrees

9. 90 degrees, 270 degrees

10. 180 degrees, 180 degrees

11. 120 degrees, 240 degrees

12. 60 degrees, 300 degrees

13. Together, they add up to 360 degrees.

Lesson 2.2: Plane Surfaces

1. Many possible answers: Planes do not exist on Earth; nothing can exist here that goes on forever because Earth does not go on forever in any direction.
2. Cannot be done
3. Many possible answers: A figure that has a specific length and width cannot contain lines, which go on forever.
4. 3
5. 3
6. 3
7. 6
8. 8
9. 5

Lesson 2.3: Polygons

1.
   A. Rectangle
   B. Square
   C. Octagon
   D. Triangle

E. Hexagon
F. Triangle
G. Pentagon
H. Decagon

2. 5 shapes: b, c, d, e, h

Lesson 2.4: Tessellations

1. 6
2. Student's tesselation should look like this:

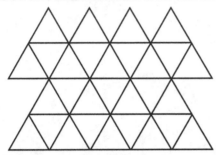

3–6.   Various possible answers: Of regular polygons, only rectangles, triangles, and hexagons tessellate because only these shapes have angles with degrees that add up evenly to 360.

7.

Shape	Yes, It Can Tessellate	No, It Cannot Tessellate
Triangle	X	
Rectangle	X	
Pentagon		X
Octagon		X
Hexagon	X	

8. Answers will vary
9. Many possible answers: Certain regular polygons tessellate because 360 degree is evenly divisible by their angle measurement.

Lesson 2.5: Tearing Triangles

1. No, they will not leave any space.

2. No
3. 60 degrees

4. 180 degrees
5. Yes
6. Yes
7. Yes
8. Yes
9. All three angles of a triangle together always add up to 180 degrees.
10. The angles of a regular polygon that tessellates must add up evenly to 360 degrees.

Lesson 2.6: Translation Tessellations

1. Yes
2. Yes, there are many possible answers as to why this is true. One example: The square has been altered in a symmetrical way, so it will not change its ability to tessellate.
3. Yes
4. Yes, it has been altered in a symmetrical way.

Lesson 2.7: Rotational Symmetry Tessellation.

Check to see if student's drawing properly tessellates.

Lesson 2.8:

See rubric on p. 136 (Appendix C).

UNIT 3

Lesson 3.1: Making a Perfect Square

1. The angles wouldn't be equal.
2. Many possible answers: He could bend the rope around a tree.
3. A triangle can only have one right angle. Many possible answers: The triangle only had 180 degrees in it, (as we learned in the last unit,) so two right angles would leave nothing for the third angle; it would be too big inside.
4. Many possible answers: any triangle with 12 equal measures.

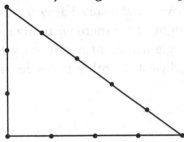

5. Answers will vary.
6.

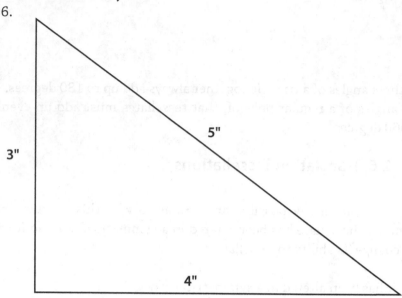

7. Yes
8. No, it cannot be done.
9. Yes
10. Yes
11. Many possible answers: Some may involve making right triangles with the string and using the right angles from the triangles to make a square. Some may involve making two diagonals with the string and from corner to corner and making sure that they are the same length.
12. Many possible answers: Each should use the same method as in Problem 10, but with bigger objects and people moving the rope. Make sure students include all the necessary steps in their answer.

Lesson 3.2: Making the Pyramid Face the Correct Way

1. Many possible answers: Thomas's solution on page 96 is a good example.
2. A shadow falls in the direction *opposite* to the source of light that casts it.
3. East
4. Several possible answers: Measure halfway across the middle of the circle and make a right angle there with one side touching east. The other side of the angle will point north or south. Or, if a square has sides facing east and west, its other two sides have to face north and south.

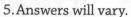

Lesson 3.3: Area of Rectangles

1. 2 cubits
2. 4 cubits
3. 8 square cubits
4. 7 cubits
5. 7 cubits
6. 49 square cubits
7. Many different answers: The length multiplied by the width equals the area.
8. L × H = A
9. No, it is not always true. Many possible answers: The height is not always equal to 2.
10. L × H = A
11. L × L = A, H × H = A, or L^2 = A

Lesson 3.4: Area of Triangles

1. 24
2. L × H/2 = A
3. Yes
4. Yes
5. Yes, it is always true.
6. Yes, the area of the triangle is half of the area of the entire rectangle.

Lesson 3.5: Surface Area of Three-Dimensional Shapes

1. L × L=A, or L^2 = A
2. L × H/2 = A
3. (L × L) + 4(L × H/2) = Surface area of pyramid
4. 28
5. 313,280 square cubits
6. 193,600 square cubits
7. 506,880 square cubits
8. Two rectangles at 4 × 5 = 20 is 40. Two rectangles at 4 × 6 = 24 is 48. Two rectangles at 6 × 5 = 30 is 60. All together, this equals 148 square inches.
9. To figure this out, students must remember the symbol for right triangles and the rule about the ratio of the sides of a right triangle. If they do, they will realize that the height of this triangle must be 4 inches (3, 4, 5 always equals the side measures of a right triangle). Because the height of the two triangles is 4, their areas are each 4 × 6/2 = 12.

The three rectangles are 10 × 6 = 60, 10 × 5 = 50, and 10 × 5 = 50. 60 + 50 + 50 = 160, 2 × 12 = 24, 160 + 24 = 184 square inches.

Lesson 3.6: Cylinder Extra Challenge

1. The area of the circle at the end is 2 × 2 × 3.14 = 12.56, and there are two of them = 25.12.
2. The side is actually a rectangle. Its height is 4"; its width is the circumference of the circle. In this case, it is again 2 × 2 × 3.14 = 12.56 × 4 = 50.24.
3. The surface area of the whole shape is therefore 75.36 square inches.

Extension

Example. My first 3-D shape was a cube. I found its surface area by adding together the areas for all the 2-D shapes that make it up. It has six squares.

The equation for the area of the first shape is A = L × W. Its measurements were $L^{2"} × W^{2"}$ so its area was 4 square inches. I multiplied that times the number of squares (6) and got 24 square inches.

Word Explanation Example. I wanted to make three three-dimensional shapes that all had exactly the same surface area. I started out by making a cube. I found its surface area by adding together the areas for all the two- dimensional shapes that make it up. A cube is made up of six squares. A square's area is its length times its width, or, because they are the same, its length times itself. I made my squares with a length of 2 inches each so I knew each square was 2" × 2", which equaled 4 square inches. There were six squares and so the surface area was 24 square inches.

Note: In addition to writing a paragraph similar to this for each shape, students must explain how they went about making sure that the shapes had equal surface area. Did they use guess and check? Did they figure out a relationship between the shapes' surface areas mathematically?

APPENDIX C

SELECTED RUBRICS

Name: _____ Date: _____

RUBRIC: MAKING A GIANT OBJECT

CATEGORY	4	3	2	1	Score
Details	Giant object details are all easily viewed and identifiable from across the classroom.	Most giant object details are easily viewed and identifiable from across the classroom.	Most giant object details are easily identified when the object is seen close-up.	Many giant object details are not clear.	
Ratio and Construction	The student can clearly describe the steps used to make his or her giant object. The student can accurately point out how this process used ratio.	The student can clearly describe the steps used to make his or her giant object. The student can mostly explain how this process used ratio.	The student can describe most of the steps used to make his or her giant object. The student can sort of explain how this process used ratio.	The student has great difficulty describing the steps used to construct his or her giant object. The student can't explain how this process used ratio.	
Attractiveness/ Craftsmanship	The object shows that the creator was took great pride in his or her work. The design and construction look carefully planned. The item is neat.	The object shows that the creator took pride in his or her work. The design and construction look planned. The item has a few flaws, but these do not detract from the overall look.	The design and construction were planned. The item has several flaws, that detract from the overall look.	The object looks thrown together at the last minute. It appears that little design or planning was done. Craftsmanship is poor.	
Time and Effort	Class time was used wisely. Much time and effort went into the planning and design of the object.	Class time was used wisely.	Class time was not always used wisely.	Class time was not used wisely.	
Working With Others	Almost always listens to, shares with, and supports the efforts of others. Tries to keep people working well together.	Usually listens to, shares with, and supports the efforts of others. Does not cause "waves" in the group.	Often listens to, shares with, and supports the efforts of others, but sometimes is not a good team member.	Rarely listens to, shares with, and supports the efforts of others. Often is not a good team player.	
				Total	

Time-Travel Math © Prufrock Press • Permission is granted to photocopy or reproduce this page for classroom use only.

Name: _____ Date: _____

RUBRIC: MODEL CLASSROOM

CATEGORY	Weight for Each Category	4	3	2	1
Accuracy	× 3 (up to 12 points available)	95% or more of the structure is drawn accurately and is recognizable. Ratios are nearly all correct.	80% or more of the structure is drawn accurately and is recognizable. Ratios are mostly all correct.	70% or more of the structure is drawn accurately and is recognizable. Some of the ratios are correct.	Less than 60% of the structure is drawn accurately. Many ratio mistakes.
Drawing—general	× 1 (up to 4 points available)	Lines are clear and not smudged. There are almost no erasures or stray marks on the paper. Overall, the quality of the drawing is excellent.	There are a few erasures, smudged lines, or stray marks on the paper, but they do not greatly detract from the drawing. Overall, the drawing is good.	There are a few erasures, smudged lines, or stray marks on the paper, which detract from the drawing. Overall, the quality of the drawing is fair.	There are several erasures, smudged lines, or stray marks on the paper, which detract from the drawing. Overall, the quality of the drawing is poor.
Knowledge Gained	× 2 (up to 8 points available)	When asked about items in the drawing, student knows the size and how it was determined.	When asked about items in the drawing, student knows the size of most and how it was determined.	When asked about items in the drawing, student knows the size of some and how it was determined.	When asked about items in the r drawing, student knows the size of a few, but not how it was determined.
Cooperation	× 1 (up to 4 points available)	Worked very well with the group and contributed a great deal to the project.	Worked with the group and contributed to the project.	Worked with the group and contributed somewhat to the project.	Didn't work very well with the group and/ or contributed little to the project.
Labels	× 1 (up to 4 points available)	Every item that needs to be identified has a label. It is clear which label goes with which structure.	Almost all items that need to be identified have labels. It is clear which label goes with which structure.	Most items that need to be identified have labels. It is clear which label goes with which structure.	Less than 75% of the items that need to be identified have labels OR it is not clear which label goes with which item.
				Total	

Name: _____ Date: _____

RUBRIC: FINAL TESSELLATION PROJECT

CATEGORY	4	3	2	1
Time and Effort	Class time was used wisely. Much time and effort went into the planning and design of the tessellation. It is clear the student worked at home as well as at school.	Class time was used wisely. Student could have put in more time and effort at home.	Class time was not always used wisely, but student did do some additional work at home.	Class time was not used wisely and the student put in no additional effort.
Understanding of Media	The student can define the term tessellation and tell how it differs from other designs. His or her understanding is shown in the artwork.	The student can define the term tessellation and tell how it differs from other designs.	The student can kind of define the term tessellation and tell how it differs from other designs.	The student has trouble defining the term tessellation and describing how it differs from other designs.
Creativity	Several of the graphics or objects used in the collage reflect an exceptional degree of student creativity in their creation and/or display.	One or two of the graphics or objects used in the collage reflect student creativity in their creation and/or display.	One or two graphics or objects were made or customized by the student, but the ideas were typical rather than creative.	The student did not customize any of the items on the collage.
Quality of Construction	The tessellation shows considerable attention to construction. The items are neatly trimmed. All items are carefully and securely attached to the backing, or neatly drawn. There are no stray marks, smudges, or glue stains. Nothing is hanging over the edges.	The tessellation shows attention to construction. The items are neatly trimmed or drawn. All items are carefully and securely attached to the backing. A few barely noticeable stray marks, smudges, or glue stains are present. Nothing is hanging over the edges.	The tessellation shows some attention to construction. Most items are neatly trimmed or drawn. All items are securely attached to the backing. A few barely noticeable stray marks, smudges, or glue stains are present. Nothing is hanging over the edges.	The tessellation was put together sloppily. Items appear to be just "slapped on" or drawn quickly. Pieces may be loose or hanging over the edges. Smudges, stains, rips, uneven edges, and/or stray marks are evident.
Titles and Text	Title and text were written clearly and are easy to read from a distance. Text paragraph clearly explained what a tessellation is and some of the mathematics involved.	Title and text were written clearly and are easy to read close-up. Text paragraph explained what a tessellation is and some of the mathematics involved.	Titles and text were written clearly and are easy to read close-up. There was little variation in the appearance of text. Text paragraph sort of explained what a tessellation is.	Titles and/or text are hard to read, even when the reader is close. No real explanation of tessellations or math included.
			Total	

REFERENCES

Escher, M. C. (1958). *Regelmatige vlakverdeling (Regular division of the plane)*. Utrecht, The Netherlands: Foundation de Roos.

National Council of Teachers of Mathematics. (2000). *Principles and standards for school mathematics.* Reston, VA: Author.

Winebrenner, S. (2001). *Teaching gifted kids in the regular classroom: Strategies and techniques every teacher can use to meet the academic needs of the gifted and talented* (Rev. ed.). Minneapolis, MN: Free Spirit.

ABOUT THE AUTHOR

Amy Bernstein studied gifted education at the University of Virginia, receiving her master's degree in education there in 1989. Since that time, she has run gifted programs in Waltham and Pepperell, MA, and has taught and tutored gifted students. Ms. Bernstein was the first teacher in the state of Massachusetts to be certified in academically advanced education. She lives in Framingham, MA, with her husband and two daughters, her dog, her two cats, her lizard, and her turtle.

Printed in the United States
by Baker & Taylor Publisher Services

Printed in the United States
by Baker & Taylor Publisher Services